Other books by the author

Non fiction

1. Break Away from the Chains of **Limiting Beliefs** ...to Soar High up in the Sky

Fiction

1. The foul smelling man on a train: 26 short stories: A cocktail of emotions
2. A cocktail of emotions 2 : Summer Rains

Unlock the **POWER** of **NEUROPLASTICITY:** Learn to **REWIRE** your brain for lifelong **GROWTH**

Disclaimer

The content of this book is for informational and educational purposes only. The author has made every effort to ensure the accuracy and completeness of the information provided. However, this book is not intended as a substitute for professional advice or therapy. The reader should consult a qualified professional before taking any action based on the information provided in this book. The author and publisher disclaim any liability arising directly or indirectly from the use or application of any of the contents of this book.

Copyright © 2024 KV Shan

All rights reserved. No part of this book may be reproduced, stored in a retrieval system, or transmitted in any form or by any means—electronic, mechanical, photocopying, recording, or otherwise—without the prior written permission of the author, except in the case of brief quotations embodied in critical articles or reviews.

Published by KV Shan

ISBN: 9798303292819

First Edition: Dec 2024

For more information, please contact
kvshan23@gmail.com

Author's note

Dear Reader,

Thank you for joining me on this transformative journey into the world of neuroplasticity. As a passionate storyteller and an explorer of the mind, I've dedicated my writing to uncovering the profound framework that shapes our thoughts, beliefs, and actions.

In this book, I delve deep into the incredible ability of our brains to adapt, evolve, and change—regardless of age or circumstance. Throughout my journey, I have come to realize that the real power lies not just in our experiences, but in how we choose to perceive them.

My previous works have been rooted in the exploration of limiting beliefs, and it's through overcoming these barriers that we unlock the potential for growth and transformation. Neuroplasticity is the key that allows us to reshape our narratives, challenge the status quo, and ultimately rewrite our stories.

I invite you to open your mind to the possibilities that lie within the pages ahead. Let this book inspire you to harness the power of your mind, embrace change, and embark on a new path toward self-discovery and empowerment.

Together, let's unlock the extraordinary potential of our brains.

With gratitude and excitement,

KV Shan

Table of contents

1. Introduction to Neuroplasticity...14

2. The Brain's Architecture..14

3. Types of Neuroplasticity..15

4. Mechanisms of Neuroplasticity...15

5. Neuroplasticity in Learning and Memory/6............................15

6. The Role of Neuroplasticity in Recovery from Injury...............16

7. Neuroplasticity and Recovery from Brain Injury......................16

8. Neuroplasticity across the Lifespan..16

9. Neuroplasticity in Mental Health..17

10. Neuroplasticity and learning...17

11. Harnessing neuroplasticity with age progression....................18

12. Neuroplasticity in the Age of Technology..................................18

13. The Future of Neuroplasticity...18

14. Conclusion... 18

Chapter summaries

Chapter 1: Introduction to Neuroplasticity...................................20

Chapter 2: The Brain's Architecture..25

Chapter 3: Types of Neuroplasticity..29

Chapter 4: Mechanisms of Neuroplasticity..................................31

Chapter 5: Neuroplasticity in Learning and Memory..................42

Chapter 6: The Role of Neuroplasticity in Recovery from Injury..46

Chapter 7: Neuroplasticity and Recovery from Brain Injury......53

Chapter 8: Neuroplasticity across the Lifespan..........................59

Chapter 9: Neuroplasticity and Mental Health............................63

Chapter 10: Neuroplasticity and Learning...................................71

Chapter 11: Harnessing Neuroplasticity with age progression...80

Chapter 12: Neuroplasticity in the Age of Technology.................91

Chapter 13: The Future of Neuroplasticity....................................98

Chapter 14: Conclusion..104

The Boundless Potential of Neuroplasticity................................104

Chapter summaries

1. **Introduction to Neuroplasticity**

In this opening chapter, let's define neuroplasticity and explore its history in scientific research. The idea that the brain can change and adapt throughout life contradicts earlier beliefs that the brain's structure is fixed after childhood. This section will lay the groundwork by explaining why neuroplasticity is a revolutionary concept in neuroscience such as

What is Neuroplasticity?

The Historical Context of Neuroplasticity

The Science behind Brain Plasticity

The Importance of Neuroplasticity in Modern Neuroscience

2. **The Brain's Architecture**

This chapter delves into the physical structure of the brain, focusing on neurons, synapses, and neurotransmitters that facilitate communication between brain cells. It will also introduce the reader to how neuroplastic changes happen at the cellular level.

Overview of Brain Anatomy

Neurons: The Building Blocks of the Brain

Synapses and Neural Connections

Role of Neurotransmitters in Plasticity

3. Types of Neuroplasticity

Neuroplasticity can be categorized into several types, such as structural and functional plasticity. This chapter will cover these types in detail, explaining how they influence our ability to learn new skills, recover from injury, and adapt to new environments and the categories would be

Structural Neuroplasticity

Functional Neuroplasticity

Synaptic Plasticity

Non-Synaptic Plasticity

4. Mechanisms of Neuroplasticity

Understanding the mechanisms behind neuroplasticity helps explain how the brain strengthens or weakens neural connections. The chapter covers processes like Long-Term Potentiation (LTP) and Long-Term Depression (LTD), as well as the roles of neurogenesis and synaptic pruning.

Long-Term Potentiation (LTP)

Long-Term Depression (LTD)

Neurogenesis: The Birth of New Neurons

Pruning: The Brain's Efficiency Mechanism

5. Neuroplasticity in Learning and Memory

Here, we explore how the brain forms new memories and learns new skills. The brain's ability to adapt through neuroplasticity allows it to strengthen neural pathways that support learning and cognitive function.

How the Brain Learns

Strengthening Neural Pathways

The Role of Neuroplasticity in Memory Formation

Skill Acquisition and Plasticity

6. The Role of Neuroplasticity in Recovery from Injury

When the brain or spinal cord is injured, neuroplasticity is the mechanism through which recovery is possible. This chapter will explain how the brain reorganizes itself after damage and the rehabilitation techniques that enhance this process.

Brain Recovery after Stroke

Recovery from Traumatic Brain Injuries (TBI)

Spinal Cord Injuries and Neuroplastic Adaptations

Rehabilitation Techniques Leveraging Plasticity

7. Neuroplasticity and Recovery from Brain Injury

Neuroplasticity plays a crucial role in the brain's ability to recover from injuries such as trauma, stroke, or traumatic brain injury (TBI). It enables the brain to reorganize and form new neural connections to compensate for lost functions.

Recovery in Specific Injuries

Factors Affecting Recovery

8. Neuroplasticity across the Lifespan

Neuroplasticity, the brain's ability to reorganize and form new connections, occurs throughout life, though it varies at different stages.

Infancy and early childhood

Adolescence

Adulthood

Older Age

Factors such as environmental enrichment, exercise, sleep, diet, and stress management influence neuroplasticity throughout life.

9. Neuroplasticity in Mental Health

This chapter explores the impact of neuroplasticity on mental health conditions, including depression, anxiety, PTSD, and addiction. Understanding the brain's adaptability provides insights into therapeutic approaches that can help reshape negative patterns.

Depression and Neuroplasticity

Anxiety Disorders and Brain Adaptation

Neuroplasticity in Post-Traumatic Stress Disorder (PTSD)

The Brain's Adaptation in Addiction

10. Neuroplasticity and learning

Lifelong Learning: Engaging in continuous education and skill development keeps the brain flexible and adaptable at all ages.

Physical Exercise: Regular physical activity stimulates the production of growth factors that support neurogenesis and brain plasticity.

Mindfulness and Meditation: Practices that promote mental clarity and emotional regulation enhance neuroplasticity by strengthening focus, memory, and resilience.

Social Engagement: Maintaining strong social connections and participating in group activities encourages brain health and emotional well-being.

11. Harnessing neuroplasticity with age progression
Structural changes in brain
Enhancing neuroplasticity
Strategies

12. Neuroplasticity in the Age of Technology
Technology has both positive and negative effects on brain plasticity. In this chapter, we'll examine the implications of digital learning, social media, and innovations like virtual reality on the brain's structure and function.

The Impact of Technology on Brain Plasticity

Digital Learning and Brain Development

Social Media and Attention Span

Virtual Reality and Cognitive Enhancement

13. The Future of Neuroplasticity
Looking ahead, we explore emerging technologies and discoveries that promise to enhance our understanding of neuroplasticity, such as brain-computer interfaces and the role of artificial intelligence in fostering cognitive development.

Advances in Brain-Computer Interfaces (BCIs)

Neuroplasticity and Artificial Intelligence

Potential of Neuroplasticity in Treating Neurological Disorders

Ethical Considerations in Neuroplasticity Research

14. Conclusion
The final chapter summarizes the key takeaways from the book, emphasizing the potential of neuroplasticity in shaping our lives and the limitless opportunities for brain

growth. It also offers practical tips for continuing to support neuroplasticity in everyday life.

Recap of Neuroplasticity's Role in Human Potential

The Endless Possibilities of a Plastic Brain

How to Embrace and Foster Neuroplasticity in Daily Life

Chapter 1: Introduction to Neuroplasticity

Etymology

The word **neuroplasticity** is derived from the words neuron and plasticity. ***Neuron*** refers to the nerve cells in the brain and ***Plasticity*** comes from the Latin word plasticus which means "for moulding or modelling".

What is Neuroplasticity?

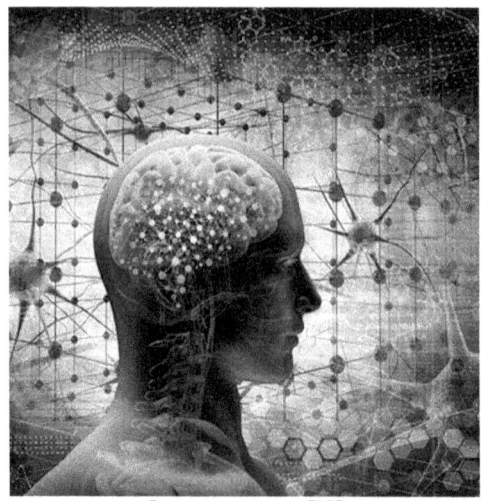
Image courtesy: CNS

Neuroplasticity, also known as brain plasticity, refers to the brain's ability to reorganize itself by forming new neural connections throughout life. It challenges the long-held belief that the adult brain is static and unchangeable after a certain age. Instead, neuroplasticity demonstrates that the brain is dynamic, constantly adapting to new experiences, learning processes, and even injuries. This ability to adapt is what allows humans to learn new skills, recover from brain injuries, and adjust to changing environments.

Neuroplasticity can happen at multiple levels, ranging from cellular changes, where individual neurons strengthen or weaken connections, to large-scale cortical remapping, where entire regions of the brain adjust in response to changes in sensory input or damage. The concept underscores that our brains are not hard-wired but rather "soft-wired" and constantly evolving.

The Historical Context of Neuroplasticity

Let's look into a brief chronology on the concept of neuroplasticity and it's evolution. The concept of neuroplasticity, or the idea that the brain can change throughout life, has a long history that dates back to the late 1800s

1793
Italian anatomist Michele Vicenzo Malacarne conducted one of the first experiments that provided evidence of neuroplasticity.

1890
Psychologist William James used the term "plasticity" in his book The Principles of Psychology to describe the brain's ability to change in response to influences.

1923
Karl Lashley conducted experiments on rhesus monkeys that demonstrated changes in neuronal pathways.

1948
Polish neuroscientist Jerzy Konorski first used the term "neuroplasticity" to describe changes in neuronal structure.

1910–1941

Psychiatrist Adolf Meyer at Johns Hopkins University was influential in translating the concept of plasticity into a framework for clinical psychiatry.

Before the 1960s, researchers believed that the brain's physical structure was mostly permanent and that changes could only occur during infancy and childhood.

The idea that the brain can change and adapt is relatively new in neuroscience. For centuries, scientists believed that brain development was completed in early childhood and that after a certain point, the brain became rigid, incapable of growth or adaptation. This perspective was rooted in the work of 19th-century scientists like Santiago Ramón y Cajal, who famously described the adult brain as being unable to regenerate or reorganize itself.

However, in the mid-20th century, new research began to challenge this view. In the 1960s, neuroscientist Paul Bach-y-Rita's research showed that the brain could compensate for sensory loss, sparking the modern field of neuroplasticity. By the 1990s, technological advancements like functional MRI (fMRI) and positron emission tomography (PET) scans allowed scientists to observe real-time changes in the brain, confirming that neuroplasticity was a lifelong process.

Today, neuroplasticity is widely accepted as a fundamental principle of how the brain works, with applications ranging from education to rehabilitation medicine.

The Science behind brain plasticity

The biological basis of neuroplasticity lies in the brain's neurons—specialized cells that transmit information. Neurons are connected to one another through synapses, the junctions where electrical or chemical signals pass. The strength of these connections determines how effectively information is processed in the brain.

When we learn new information, practice a skill, or adapt to changes, neurons undergo structural and functional changes. This occurs in several ways:

Strengthening synaptic connections: Repeated activation of a neural pathway reinforces synaptic connections, making them more efficient.

Creating new synapses: New experiences can prompt the brain to form new connections between neurons, facilitating learning and adaptation.

Pruning unused connections: The brain eliminates weak or unused synaptic connections, a process known as synaptic pruning, which improves efficiency.

These processes collectively ensure that the brain remains flexible and capable of responding to the demands of learning and environmental changes.

Image courtesy Cleaveland Clinic

The importance of Neuroplasticity in modern neuroscience

Neuroplasticity is a cornerstone of modern neuroscience because it explains how the brain can learn and recover from damage. It helps to understand how individuals can improve their cognitive function through learning or rehabilitation, despite aging or injury. Neuroplasticity plays a key role in many areas:

Learning and memory: Neuroplasticity is the mechanism by which we acquire new knowledge, form memories, and develop skills.

Recovery from injury: After brain damage (from a stroke, traumatic injury, or neurodegenerative disease), neuroplasticity helps the brain reorganize itself to compensate for lost functions.

Mental health treatment: Understanding neuroplasticity has led to new approaches in treating mental health disorders such as depression and anxiety, where rewiring negative thought patterns through therapy can lead to recovery.

Research into neuroplasticity has also opened doors to exciting new fields like brain-computer interfaces, neural prosthetics, and cognitive enhancement therapies, all of which have the potential to revolutionize how we interact with our brains.

You shall find a little bit of jargonic literature here onward but unfortunately technical terms can't be broken down further any better than this.

Chapter 2: The Brain's Architecture

To know more about neuro plasticity we need to know a little more about our brain.

Overview of brain anatomy

The brain is a complex organ that consists of billions of neurons working together to process information and control bodily functions. At a basic level, the brain is divided into three main areas: the cerebrum, the cerebellum, and the brainstem.

Cerebrum: This is the largest part of the brain, divided into two hemispheres (left and right) and responsible for higher-order functions such as thought, reasoning, emotion, and voluntary movement. Each hemisphere has four lobes: the frontal, parietal, occipital, and temporal lobes, each responsible for different functions such as motor control, sensory perception, vision, and hearing.

Cerebellum: Located beneath the cerebrum, the cerebellum is responsible for coordinating movement and maintaining balance.

Brainstem: The brainstem controls basic life functions such as breathing, heartbeat, and blood pressure.

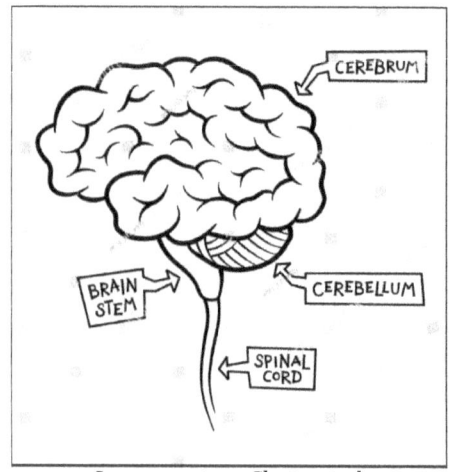

Image courtesy: Shutterstock

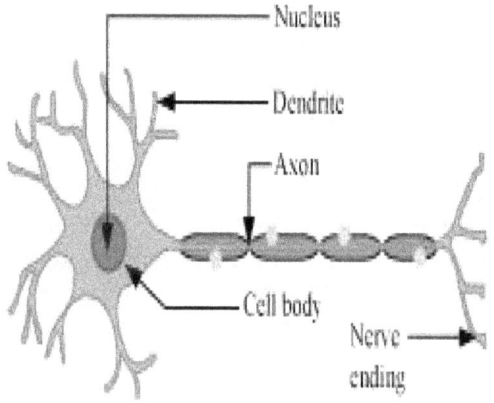

Image courtesy: Byju's

Neurons: The Building Blocks of the Brain

Neurons, or nerve cells, are the fundamental units of the brain and nervous system. They are specialized to transmit information throughout the body. Each neuron has three primary parts:

Cell body (soma): The cell body contains the nucleus and is responsible for maintaining the cell's functions.

Dendrites: Dendrites are tree-like structures that receive signals from other neurons and relay them to the cell body.

Axon: The axon carries signals away from the cell body to other neurons, muscles, or glands. Axons can vary in length from a fraction of a millimeter to several feet.

Neurons communicate with each other through electrical impulses and chemical signals at synapses, which are the junctions between neurons.

Synapses and neural connections

A synapse is the point where one neuron communicates with another. At the synapse, an electrical impulse triggers the release of neurotransmitters (chemical messengers) from the axon terminal of the presynaptic neuron. These neurotransmitters cross the synaptic gap and bind to receptors on the postsynaptic neuron's dendrites, either exciting or inhibiting the next neuron from firing an electrical impulse.

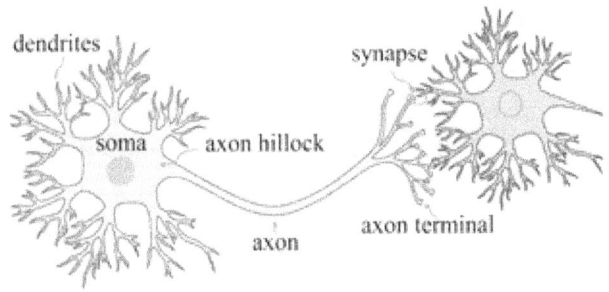

Image courtesy ReaearchGate

There are two primary types of synapses:

Excitatory synapses: Increase the likelihood that the next neuron will fire an electrical signal.

Inhibitory synapses: Decrease the likelihood of the next neuron firing.

The strength and number of synaptic connections between neurons are key factors in neuroplasticity, as they determine how information is transmitted and processed in the brain.

Role of Neurotransmitters in plasticity

Neurotransmitters play a crucial role in regulating neuroplasticity by transmitting signals between neurons. Different neurotransmitters have varying effects on brain function. Examples of a few of the neurotransmitters are

Glutamate: The primary excitatory neurotransmitter, essential for synaptic plasticity, learning, and memory.

GABA (gamma-aminobutyric acid): The primary inhibitory neurotransmitter, which helps prevent overexcitement in the brain and maintains balance in neural activity.

Dopamine: Involved in reward, motivation, and reinforcement learning, dopamine influences neuroplasticity by affecting the brain's ability to form and strengthen synaptic connections.

Serotonin: A neurotransmitter that affects mood, emotion, and cognition. Serotonin can modulate plasticity, particularly in areas related to emotional regulation.

The balance of neurotransmitters is vital for optimal brain function, and disturbances in this balance can lead to mental health issues or cognitive dysfunction.

Chapter 3: Types of Neuroplasticity

Structural Neuroplasticity

Structural neuroplasticity refers to the physical changes in the brain's structure, typically in response to learning or environmental changes. This type of plasticity involves:

Growth of new dendrites: When a person learns something new or has repeated experiences, neurons can grow new dendrites, increasing their ability to receive and process information.

Increased synapse density: The creation of new synapses (synaptogenesis) strengthens connections between neurons, allowing for more efficient communication.

For example, studies have shown that London taxi drivers, who memorize complex city maps, have an enlarged hippocampus (the brain area associated with spatial memory) due to structural neuroplasticity.

Functional Neuroplasticity

Functional neuroplasticity refers to the brain's ability to shift functions from damaged areas to undamaged areas. This is particularly important in recovery from brain injuries, such as strokes or traumatic injuries. The brain can "reassign" tasks normally handled by damaged regions to healthy areas, allowing individuals to regain lost functions.

For instance, stroke patients often regain the ability to speak or move affected limbs through intensive rehabilitation, during which functional plasticity allows the brain to rewire itself.

Synaptic plasticity

Synaptic plasticity is the brain's ability to strengthen or weaken synapses in response to activity levels. This type of plasticity is the basis of learning and memory. Two primary mechanisms of synaptic plasticity are:

Long-Term Potentiation (LTP): Strengthens synaptic connections after repeated activation, making future signal transmission more efficient.

Long-Term Depression (LTD): Weakens synaptic connections when they are underutilized, allowing the brain to prioritize more active connections.

Non-Synaptic plasticity

Non-synaptic plasticity refers to changes in the intrinsic properties of neurons themselves, independent of synaptic changes. These alterations affect how neurons respond to incoming signals, influencing overall brain function. Non-synaptic plasticity can affect ion channel expression, membrane properties, or the overall excitability of neurons.

Chapter 4: Mechanisms of Neuroplasticity

Neuroplasticity encompasses a variety of mechanisms that enable the brain to adapt, reorganize, and form new connections in response to experiences, learning, and injury. Understanding these mechanisms is crucial for appreciating how the brain maintains its functionality and adaptability throughout life. This chapter delves into the primary mechanisms that facilitate neuroplastic changes, including Long-Term Potentiation (LTP), Long-Term Depression (LTD), neurogenesis, and synaptic pruning.

Long-Term Potentiation (LTP)

Long-Term Potentiation (LTP) is one of the most extensively studied mechanisms underlying synaptic plasticity. It refers to the long-lasting strengthening of synapses based on recent patterns of activity. LTP is considered a cellular correlate of learning and memory.

1. Mechanism of LTP:

Synaptic Activation: LTP is typically induced by a high-frequency stimulation of presynaptic neurons, which leads to a sustained depolarization of the postsynaptic neuron.

NMDA receptor activation: During this process, N-Methyl-D-Aspartate (NMDA) receptors, a type of glutamate receptor, become activated. These receptors are both ligand-gated and voltage-dependent, requiring both glutamate binding and postsynaptic depolarization to allow calcium ions (Ca^{2+}) to enter the neuron.

Calcium influx: The influx of Ca^{2+} into the postsynaptic neuron triggers a cascade of intracellular events, including the activation of protein kinases such as Ca²⁺/calmodulin-dependent protein kinase II (CaMKII).

AMPA receptor insertion: One of the critical outcomes of this cascade is the insertion of more α-amino-3-hydroxy-5-methyl-4-isoxazolepropionic acid (AMPA) receptors into the postsynaptic membrane, increasing the neuron's sensitivity to glutamate.

Structural changes: Over time, LTP can lead to the growth of new dendritic spines and synaptic connections, reinforcing the synaptic strength.

2. Functional significance of LTP:

Learning and Memory: LTP is essential for the formation of long-term memories. By strengthening synaptic connections, the brain can store information more effectively.

Synaptic Efficiency: Enhanced synaptic transmission ensures that neural circuits involved in specific tasks become more efficient, facilitating quicker and more robust responses.

3. Experimental evidence:

Hippocampal Studies: The hippocampus, a brain region critical for memory formation, has been a primary site for studying LTP. Experiments involving electrical stimulation of the hippocampal pathways have consistently demonstrated the induction and maintenance of LTP.

Behavioral Correlations: Behavioral studies in animals have shown that disrupting LTP impairs learning and memory tasks, further supporting its role in cognitive functions.

Long-Term Depression (LTD)

Long-Term Depression (LTD) is the counterpart to LTP, involving the long-lasting weakening of synaptic strength.

LTD is equally important for maintaining synaptic plasticity and overall neural network stability.

1. Mechanism of LTD:

Low-Frequency stimulation: Unlike LTP, LTD is typically induced by prolonged low-frequency stimulation of presynaptic neurons.

NMDA receptor activation: Similar to LTP, NMDA receptors play a role in LTD, but the resulting intracellular calcium levels are lower.

Calcium signalling: The modest influx of Ca^{2+} activates phosphatases, such as protein phosphatase 1 (PP1) and calcineurin, which dephosphorylate target proteins.

AMPA receptor removal: This leads to the internalization of AMPA receptors from the postsynaptic membrane, reducing synaptic sensitivity to glutamate.

Synaptic scaling: LTD contributes to synaptic scaling, a process that ensures neural circuits remain balanced by preventing overexcitation.

2. Functional significance of LTD:

Memory encoding: LTD is believed to play a role in forgetting or the clearance of irrelevant information, allowing for the fine-tuning of memory encoding.

Synaptic homeostasis: By weakening certain synapses, LTD helps maintain overall synaptic homeostasis, preventing excessive neuronal firing and maintaining network stability.

3. Experimental evidence:

Cerebellar studies: The cerebellum has been instrumental in elucidating the mechanisms of LTD. Studies involving Purkinje cells have demonstrated how LTD contributes to motor learning.

Purkinje cells, a distinctive type of neuron found exclusively in the cerebellar cortex, are known for their striking, flat dendritic trees that are extensively branched. These intricate structures enable Purkinje cells to process vast amounts of information and adapt by reshaping their dendrites, supporting their role in learning and integration.

Behavioural implications: Disruptions in LTD have been linked to impaired motor coordination and learning deficits in animal models.

Neurogenesis is the birth of new neurons which refers to the process by which new neurons are generated from neural stem cells. This process was once thought to be limited to early development, but it is now known to continue into adulthood, primarily in specific brain regions.

1. Sites of adult Neurogenesis:

Hippocampus: The dentate gyrus of the hippocampus is a primary site for adult neurogenesis, playing a crucial role in learning and memory.

Subventricular zone (SVZ): The SVZ lining the lateral ventricles generates new neurons that migrate to the olfactory bulb, contributing to the sense of smell.

2. Mechanism of Neurogenesis:

Stem Cell Proliferation: Neural stem cells divide to produce progenitor cells, which then differentiate into neurons.

Migration: Newly formed neurons migrate to their designated locations within the brain.

Integration: These neurons extend dendrites and axons, forming synaptic connections with existing neurons, thereby integrating into existing neural circuits.

3. Functional significance of Neurogenesis:

Cognitive Flexibility: Neurogenesis contributes to cognitive flexibility, enabling the brain to adapt to new information and environments.

Mood Regulation: There is evidence linking neurogenesis to mood regulation, with decreased neurogenesis associated with depression and increased neurogenesis linked to the effects of antidepressants.

Recovery and Compensation: Following brain injury, neurogenesis can aid in recovery by replacing lost neurons and restoring neural circuitry.

4. Experimental Evidence:

Animal Models: Studies in rodents have shown that factors like enriched environments, physical exercise, and learning tasks can enhance neurogenesis in the hippocampus.

Human Studies: Neuroimaging and post-mortem analyses have provided evidence of adult neurogenesis in humans, although the extent and functional significance are still under investigation.

Synaptic Pruning: The Brain's Efficiency Mechanism

Synaptic pruning is the process by which unnecessary or weak synaptic connections are eliminated, refining neural circuits for optimal efficiency and functionality. This mechanism is essential for both brain development and the maintenance of neural networks in adulthood.

1. Mechanism of Synaptic Pruning:

Activity-Dependent Selection: Synapses that are frequently used and strengthen through LTP are preserved, while those that are rarely activated are targeted for elimination.

Microglial Involvement: Microglia, the brain's immune cells, play a critical role in identifying and removing synapses during pruning.

Molecular Signals: Various molecular signals, including complement proteins and fractalkine, guide microglia in synapse elimination.

2. Functional Significance of Synaptic Pruning:

Developmental Refinement: During critical periods of development, such as childhood and adolescence, synaptic pruning refines neural circuits, enhancing cognitive and motor functions.

Maintaining Efficiency: In adulthood, synaptic pruning helps maintain neural network efficiency by removing redundant or inefficient connections.

Preventing Overexcitation: Pruning contributes to preventing overexcitation and excitotoxicity, which can lead to neuronal damage and neurodegenerative diseases.

3. Synaptic Pruning in Development:

Childhood and Adolescence: Significant synaptic pruning occurs during these stages, corresponding with improvements in cognitive abilities, such as abstract thinking and problem-solving.

Critical Periods: Certain skills, like language acquisition, are highly dependent on synaptic pruning during specific developmental windows.

4. Synaptic Pruning in Adulthood:

Experience-Dependent Plasticity: Even in adulthood, experiences and learning can influence which synapses are maintained or pruned, allowing for continual adaptation.

Neurodegenerative Diseases: Abnormal synaptic pruning has been implicated in various neurodegenerative and psychiatric disorders, including Alzheimer's disease and schizophrenia.

5. Experimental Evidence:

Developmental Studies: Research in animal models has demonstrated the timing and necessity of synaptic pruning for normal brain development.

Imaging Studies: Neuroimaging techniques in humans have provided insights into the patterns of synaptic pruning during different life stages, correlating with cognitive and behavioral changes.

Interplay of Mechanisms in Neuroplasticity

The mechanisms of neuroplasticity do not operate in isolation but are interconnected, working in concert to facilitate the brain's adaptability.

1. Balancing LTP and LTD:

Homeostatic Plasticity: The balance between LTP and LTD ensures that synaptic strengths remain within optimal ranges, preventing runaway excitation or depression.

Synaptic Scaling: This process adjusts the overall synaptic strengths to stabilize neural network activity, maintaining functional equilibrium.

2. Integration of Neurogenesis and Synaptic Pruning:

Circuit Integration: Newly generated neurons integrate into existing circuits, and synaptic pruning refines these connections to enhance circuit efficiency.

Experience-Dependent Adaptation: Experiences can influence both neurogenesis and synaptic pruning, allowing the brain to adapt structurally and functionally to new demands.

3. Role of Neurotransmitters and Signaling Pathways:

Modulatory Effects: Neurotransmitters like dopamine and serotonin modulate the processes of LTP, LTD, neurogenesis, and synaptic pruning, influencing overall neuroplastic outcomes.

Intracellular Cascades: Signaling pathways activated by neurotransmitter receptors coordinate the molecular events necessary for synaptic and structural changes.

Implications of Neuroplastic Mechanisms

Understanding the mechanisms of neuroplasticity has profound implications for various fields, including education, rehabilitation, and mental health.

1. Educational strategies:

Optimizing Learning: Insights into LTP and synaptic plasticity can inform teaching methods that enhance learning efficiency and memory retention.

Personalized Education: Recognizing individual differences in neuroplastic responses can lead to personalized educational approaches that cater to unique learning styles.

2. Rehabilitation and Recovery:

Post-Injury rehabilitation: Knowledge of functional neuroplasticity guides the development of rehabilitation programs that promote the reorganization of neural circuits to regain lost functions.

Stroke Recovery: Techniques such as constraint-induced movement therapy leverage neuroplastic mechanisms to improve motor function after a stroke.

Pruning: The brain's efficiency mechanism

Pruning is a vital aspect of neuroplasticity, especially in the early stages of brain development but also continuing throughout life. Synaptic pruning refers to the process by which the brain eliminates weak, redundant, or unused synaptic connections, allowing the brain to become more efficient by focusing resources on the most important and frequently used pathways. This refinement of neural circuits helps optimize brain function and cognitive efficiency.

Pruning is often compared to the trimming of branches from a tree—by cutting away the excess, the tree (or in this case, the brain) can grow stronger and more efficiently.

When Does Pruning Occur?

Pruning occurs throughout life but is most intense during two critical periods:

Early childhood: In the first few years of life, the brain forms a massive number of synapses—more than it will ever need. By age two or three, a child's brain has about twice as many synapses as an adult's brain. This excess provides the foundation for learning and adaptability. Between early childhood and adolescence, the brain prunes away about 50% of these synapses, focusing on those that are frequently used and strengthening them.

Adolescence: A second wave of synaptic pruning occurs during adolescence. This period is critical for refining cognitive and emotional regulation skills as the brain matures into adulthood. Pruning during this time helps optimize neural pathways for complex cognitive tasks like decision-making, problem-solving, and social interaction.

In adulthood, pruning continues on a smaller scale, allowing the brain to remain flexible and adapt to new experiences or changes in the environment.

How does Pruning work?

Pruning is driven by the principle of "use it or lose it." Synapses that are actively engaged and used frequently become stronger, while those that are rarely used become weaker and are eventually eliminated. This allows the brain to conserve energy and resources, maintaining only the most essential and efficient neural connections.

The process of pruning involves several mechanisms:

Reduction of neurotransmitter receptors: Synapses that are not frequently activated reduce the number of receptors available to receive signals, making the synaptic connection weaker.

Microglial activity: Microglia, the brain's immune cells, play a role in identifying and eliminating weak or inactive synapses. They "prune" away these connections, ensuring the brain's networks are kept efficient.

Structural changes: The dendritic spines (small protrusions on dendrites where synapses form) can retract or be eliminated altogether, physically removing the synapse.

The role of pruning in learning and development

Pruning helps the brain specialize in the skills and knowledge that are most important for an individual's environment and experiences. For example:

Language acquisition: In infancy, the brain is capable of learning any language, but as a child is exposed to their native language, the brain begins to prune synapses related to the sounds and structures of other languages. This allows the child to become more efficient at processing their native language.

Motor skills: Children initially develop a broad range of motor abilities. As they grow, pruning refines these abilities, allowing the child to excel at specific skills, such as walking, running, or writing, while less-used motor pathways are pruned away.

In adulthood, pruning helps fine-tune cognitive skills and adapt to new tasks or challenges. It ensures that the brain remains capable of learning and adaptation, even as it becomes more efficient in its processes.

Pruning and Neuroplasticity in aging

As people age, pruning continues to play a role in maintaining cognitive health. However, the process of pruning can sometimes become dysregulated, leading to cognitive decline. Conditions such as Alzheimer's disease are characterized by excessive synaptic loss, which impairs communication between neurons and leads to memory loss and cognitive impairment.

On the other hand, continued engagement in learning and cognitive activities can help maintain a healthy level of pruning, keeping the brain flexible and adaptable well into old age.

Pruning and mental health

Imbalances in pruning processes have also been linked to certain mental health conditions:

Schizophrenia: Research suggests that excessive pruning during adolescence may be a factor in the development of schizophrenia. The loss of too many synapses, particularly in the prefrontal cortex (responsible for decision-making and executive function), could contribute to the cognitive deficits and disorganized thinking associated with the disorder.

Autism spectrum disorder (ASD): In contrast, studies suggest that in some individuals with ASD, pruning may be reduced, resulting in an overabundance of synapses. This may lead to hypersensitivity to sensory input and difficulties in social interaction.

Chapter 5: Neuroplasticity in Learning and Memory

How the brain learns

Learning, at its core, is a process of neuroplasticity. Every time we learn something new, whether it's a fact, skill, or habit, our brain undergoes changes in its structure and function. Neuroplasticity allows us to form new neural pathways, strengthen existing ones, and prune away those that are no longer useful.

The process of learning typically involves three stages:

1. Acquisition: The initial stage where new information or a skill is encountered. This could be learning to play an instrument, mastering a mathematical concept, or acquiring a new language.

2. Consolidation: The information or skill is then reinforced through repetition and practice. During this stage, the neural pathways involved become stronger, making the knowledge or skill more permanent. Consolidation often occurs during sleep, when the brain processes and stores information.

3. Recall: The ability to retrieve and apply the learned information or skill in the future. Stronger neural pathways allow for quicker and more accurate recall.

Each of these stages involves changes in synaptic strength, synapse formation, and sometimes even neurogenesis (the birth of new neurons), all of which are driven by neuroplasticity.

Strengthening neural pathways

When we repeatedly perform an action or think about a piece of information, the neural pathways involved in that activity become stronger. This is the basis of habit formation and skill mastery. Repetition is key: the more frequently a pathway is activated, the more efficient the brain becomes at transmitting signals along that pathway.

For example:

Muscle memory: When you practice a physical skill, such as typing on a keyboard or playing a musical instrument, the neural pathways involved in controlling the muscles used become more efficient. Over time, the skill becomes automatic, requiring less conscious effort.

Cognitive skills: Similar to physical skills, cognitive skills such as solving math problems or playing chess involve repeated activation of specific neural pathways. With practice, these pathways become more efficient, allowing for quicker and more accurate problem-solving.

The Role of Neuroplasticity in Memory Formation

Memory is one of the clearest examples of neuroplasticity in action. When we form a memory, the brain makes structural changes to store that information. These changes include:

Synapse strengthening: The synapses between neurons involved in the memory become stronger, allowing the brain to retrieve the information more easily in the future.

New synapse formation: Sometimes, forming a memory involves creating entirely new synapses between neurons that were not previously connected.

Hippocampus involvement: The hippocampus is crucial for the formation of new memories. Neuroplasticity in this area allows us to store and recall information.

There are different types of memory, each involving neuroplasticity:

Short-term memory: Information is temporarily stored in the brain's working memory. Short-term memories are held in a limited-capacity store and are either discarded or transferred to long-term memory through consolidation.

Long-term memory: Neuroplasticity allows some short-term memories to be consolidated into long-term storage. Long-term memories are more durable and can last for days, months, or even a lifetime.

Procedural memory: This type of memory involves the retention of skills and actions, such as riding a bicycle or typing. It involves neuroplastic changes in regions like the basal ganglia and cerebellum.

Skill acquisition and plasticity

Skill acquisition is one of the most important applications of neuroplasticity. As we learn new skills, the brain reorganizes itself to accommodate the new information. This occurs through several processes:

Myelination: Repeated practice of a skill not only strengthens synaptic connections but also leads to the myelination of axons. Myelin is a fatty substance that insulates axons, allowing electrical signals to travel faster. This process speeds up communication between neurons, making skill execution more efficient.

Cortical remapping: The brain's cortex can reorganize itself based on the skills we practice. For example, when musicians practice for years, the areas of their brain responsible for hand movement and auditory processing become larger and more finely tuned.

Skill acquisition often involves a combination of synaptic plasticity, myelination, and sometimes even neurogenesis, making it a dynamic process of brain adaptation.

Chapter 6: The Role of Neuroplasticity in Recovery from Injury

Neuroplasticity plays a critical role in how the brain recovers after injury. Whether it's a traumatic brain injury (TBI), stroke, or neurological disorder, the brain has a remarkable ability to reorganize itself and compensate for lost functions. While some injuries may cause permanent damage, neuroplasticity offers the potential for functional recovery through adaptive processes.

This chapter delves into the mechanisms of how the brain recovers from injury, strategies to promote recovery, and the implications for rehabilitation and therapy.

Types of Brain Injuries and Their Impact

Before understanding the role of neuroplasticity in recovery, it is essential to grasp the different types of brain injuries and how they affect brain function. Each type of injury causes different patterns of damage and requires specific neuroplastic processes to aid recovery.

Traumatic brain injury (TBI): TBIs occur when an external force, such as a blow to the head, disrupts normal brain function. Depending on the severity, TBIs can cause localized damage (e.g., a contusion or bleeding in one part of the brain) or diffuse injury across multiple regions.

Stroke: A stroke occurs when the blood supply to a part of the brain is interrupted or reduced, preventing oxygen from reaching brain tissue. This can result in the death of brain cells in affected regions, causing loss of function such as paralysis, speech difficulties, or cognitive impairments.

Neurodegenerative disorders: Diseases like Parkinson's, Alzheimer's, and Multiple Sclerosis involve the gradual degeneration of neurons over time. Unlike acute injuries, these conditions lead to a slow, progressive loss of function.

Spinal cord injury: Although spinal cord injuries don't directly affect the brain, they disrupt communication between the brain and the rest of the body, leading to paralysis or loss of sensation. Neuroplasticity is important in helping the brain adapt to new ways of processing sensory and motor information following these injuries.

Mechanisms of recovery through Neuroplasticity

After an injury, the brain uses various neuroplastic mechanisms to compensate for lost functions. These processes can involve changes in synaptic strength, reorganization of neural circuits, and even the formation of new neurons. Let's explore some of the key mechanisms involved in recovery:

1. Functional reorganization (Cortical remapping)

One of the brain's most powerful tools for recovery is cortical remapping, in which healthy parts of the brain take over the functions of the damaged areas. After a brain injury, nearby regions may assume the responsibilities of damaged neurons through a process known as recruitment. This is especially true for injuries that affect motor or sensory functions.

For example:

Motor function: After a stroke that damages the motor cortex, neighboring areas may take on the task of controlling muscle movement in the affected limbs.

Language and speech: In cases where language centers, such as Broca's area, are damaged, nearby regions on the same or opposite hemisphere of the brain may assume language processing roles.

Functional reorganization is a gradual process and requires rehabilitation efforts like physical therapy or speech therapy to encourage new neural connections. This mechanism highlights the brain's adaptability in finding new routes to accomplish tasks once governed by the injured area.

2. Synaptogenesis

Synaptogenesis, the formation of new synapses between neurons, is a key aspect of recovery. After injury, the brain often creates new synaptic connections to reroute signals around damaged areas. These new connections can help restore communication between different brain regions and allow lost functions to re-emerge.

This process is enhanced through:

Rehabilitation exercises: Engaging in repetitive, targeted rehabilitation exercises can promote synaptogenesis by stimulating specific neural circuits.

Environmental enrichment: Exposure to novel environments and experiences can stimulate the formation of new synaptic connections.

While synaptogenesis doesn't fully replace the lost function of the damaged neurons, it helps the brain adapt by forming alternate pathways to support recovery.

3. Axonal Sprouting

Axonal sprouting refers to the growth of new branches from existing axons (the long projections of neurons). This process allows neurons to form new connections after injury, often compensating for the loss of nearby neurons. In the context of injury recovery:

Axons from surviving neurons: These neurons may grow new branches to establish connections with neurons that have lost their synaptic partners due to injury.

Long-distance connections: In some cases, axonal sprouting allows for long-distance connections, creating new communication pathways between brain regions.

Axonal sprouting is especially important in recovery from spinal cord injuries, where new pathways can help restore some degree of motor or sensory function, even if the original neural pathway remains damaged.

4. Neurogenesis in recovery

Although neurogenesis primarily occurs in the hippocampus and olfactory bulb, recent research suggests that neurogenesis may play a role in recovery after brain injury. In response to trauma, the brain may increase the production of new neurons to replace those that have been damaged or destroyed. However, the extent to which neurogenesis contributes to functional recovery in adults is still an active area of research.

Factors that promote neurogenesis after injury include:

Physical activity: Exercise has been shown to enhance neurogenesis in the hippocampus, potentially aiding in the recovery of cognitive functions after injury.

Enriched environments: Stimulating environments that promote learning and sensory engagement can enhance neurogenesis, further supporting recovery efforts.

Rehabilitation and Neuroplasticity

Rehabilitation is the cornerstone of leveraging neuroplasticity for recovery from brain injury. Physical, occupational, and cognitive therapies all work by stimulating neuroplastic changes, encouraging the brain to reorganize and compensate for lost functions.

1. Physical therapy

Physical therapy is particularly important for patients recovering from stroke, TBI, or spinal cord injury. Through repetitive motion and exercise, patients can regain strength and mobility in affected limbs. This repetitive stimulation encourages:

Motor cortex reorganization: Repetitive practice of movements helps remap the motor cortex, improving control of the affected limbs.

Strengthening of neural connections: By repeatedly activating specific neural circuits, physical therapy helps strengthen these connections and make movements more automatic.

2. Occupational therapy

Occupational therapy focuses on helping patients regain the ability to perform daily tasks such as dressing, eating, or bathing. It combines physical movement with cognitive tasks, encouraging neuroplasticity in both motor and cognitive domains.

3. Speech therapy

Speech and language impairments, common after strokes or TBIs, can benefit from neuroplastic recovery processes. Speech therapy uses repetitive exercises to promote reorganization of the language centers in the brain. In cases where the primary language center is damaged, therapy can help train the opposite hemisphere to take over language functions.

4. Cognitive rehabilitation

Cognitive rehabilitation focuses on restoring mental processes such as memory, attention, problem-solving, and executive functions. Neuroplasticity plays a key role in this, as exercises that challenge the brain encourage the formation of new neural connections. Cognitive tasks like puzzles, memory games, or problem-solving exercises help stimulate:

Neurogenesis in the hippocampus: Particularly important for memory recovery.

Strengthening of prefrontal cortex connections: Critical for improving executive functions like planning, decision-making, and multitasking.

Factors That Enhance Neuroplasticity in Recovery

Several factors can enhance the brain's ability to recover from injury by promoting neuroplastic changes:

Early intervention: The sooner rehabilitation efforts begin after an injury, the more likely the brain is to respond through neuroplastic mechanisms. Delayed therapy can lead to a reduction in the brain's adaptive capacity.

Repetitive practice: Repetition is key to reinforcing new neural pathways. Whether it's practicing a movement, a speech exercise, or a cognitive task, repetition strengthens synaptic connections, making the new behavior more automatic.

Motivation and mental engagement: Patients who are motivated and mentally engaged in their rehabilitation are more likely to experience positive outcomes. Mental engagement stimulates the brain and helps sustain the plastic changes needed for recovery.

Exercise: Regular physical exercise promotes the release of brain-derived neurotrophic factor (BDNF), a protein that supports the growth and survival of neurons, synapse formation, and overall brain health.

Sleep: Sleep plays an important role in consolidating the changes that occur during rehabilitation. During sleep, the brain processes and strengthens the neural connections formed during the day, making it critical for recovery.

Challenges and Limitations in Recovery

While neuroplasticity offers significant potential for recovery, there are limitations:

Severity of injury: In cases of severe brain damage, neuroplasticity may be insufficient to fully restore lost functions.

Aging and neuroplasticity: As the brain ages, its plasticity decreases, making recovery more difficult for older individuals.

Incomplete compensation: Even when the brain reorganizes itself to compensate for lost functions, the new pathways may not be as efficient as the original ones, leading to incomplete recovery.

Chapter 7: Neuroplasticity and Recovery from Brain Injury

Neuroplasticity plays a vital role in the brain's ability to recover from injury. Whether caused by trauma, stroke, or other neurological conditions, the brain's capacity to reorganize and rewire itself allows for the recovery of lost functions and the adaptation to new ways of operating. Understanding how neuroplasticity works in the context of brain injury offers insight into rehabilitation processes and the potential for recovery.

This chapter explores how neuroplasticity aids recovery from brain injury, the types of plastic changes that occur, and therapeutic approaches that can enhance recovery through the stimulation of neuroplasticity.

The brain's response to injury: Neuroplasticity in action

When the brain is injured, such as during a stroke or traumatic brain injury (TBI), neurons and synapses in the affected area may be damaged or destroyed. However, neuroplasticity enables the brain to compensate for this damage by recruiting new neural pathways or reorganizing existing ones.

1. Immediate and long-term plastic changes

Neuroplasticity after injury can be divided into two main phases: immediate (acute) plasticity and long-term plasticity.

Acute neuroplasticity: In the hours and days following an injury, the brain engages in rapid reorganization to limit damage and restore some basic functions. Surviving neurons adjacent to the injury site may take over functions of the damaged cells. This is the brain's natural emergency response to preserve life-sustaining functions.

Long-term neuroplasticity: Over weeks, months, and even years, the brain continues to adapt and reorganize itself. More profound structural changes occur as the brain recruits different regions or strengthens alternative pathways to compensate for the loss of the original functions.

2. Cortical Remapping

One of the most fascinating aspects of neuroplasticity following injury is cortical remapping. The cortex, the brain's outermost layer responsible for higher functions like movement, sensation, and cognition, can reorganize itself when a particular area is damaged. Nearby brain regions, or even regions from the opposite hemisphere, can take over functions previously controlled by the damaged area.

Example: In cases of stroke that damage areas responsible for motor control on one side of the body, the unaffected hemisphere of the brain may help restore movement by forming new connections. Over time, with rehabilitation, this process allows individuals to regain some or even all lost motor function.

Neuroplasticity and stroke recovery

Stroke, which occurs when blood flow to the brain is interrupted, is one of the leading causes of brain injury. The resulting damage can affect motor function, speech, cognition, and more. Recovery from stroke relies heavily on neuroplasticity.

1. Motor function recovery

Motor impairments are common after a stroke, particularly affecting one side of the body. Through neuroplasticity, the brain can compensate for this damage by recruiting alternative motor pathways.

Constraint-Induced Movement Therapy (CIMT): CIMT is a rehabilitation technique that takes advantage of neuroplasticity. In this therapy, the unaffected limb is constrained, forcing the patient to use the affected limb. This encourages the brain to rewire itself, forming new motor pathways to control the damaged limb and improve function.

Task-specific training: Repetitive, task-oriented exercises are crucial for motor recovery, as they promote the reorganization of neural circuits. The more patients practice specific tasks, such as reaching or grasping, the more the brain strengthens connections in motor regions, improving movement over time.

2. Language and Speech Recovery (Aphasia)

Aphasia, the loss of the ability to speak or understand language, is another common consequence of stroke. Speech therapy plays a critical role in stimulating neuroplastic changes that support recovery.

Speech therapy and neuroplasticity: Through repeated practice and exercises, speech therapy helps patients form new connections in language centers of the brain or recruit alternative areas to compensate for the damaged regions. Over time, this promotes the recovery of speech and language abilities.

Non-invasive brain stimulation: Techniques such as transcranial direct current stimulation (tDCS) or repetitive transcranial magnetic stimulation (rTMS) can enhance neuroplasticity in language areas, improving the effectiveness of speech therapy.

Neuroplasticity and Traumatic Brain Injury (TBI) Recovery

Traumatic brain injury (TBI) can result from accidents, falls, or blows to the head and can affect a range of cognitive, emotional, and motor functions. Neuroplasticity offers the potential for recovery through the brain's ability to adapt to the damage.

1. Cognitive rehabilitation

Cognitive functions such as memory, attention, and problem-solving can be impaired following a TBI. Neuroplasticity enables the brain to rebuild cognitive functions by forming new connections and reinforcing alternative pathways.

Cognitive exercises: Rehabilitation programs often include cognitive exercises designed to stimulate the brain's adaptive capacities. These exercises challenge memory, attention, and executive functions, encouraging neuroplastic changes that improve cognitive abilities.

Use of technology: Virtual reality and computer-based cognitive training programs have become popular tools in TBI rehabilitation. These technologies provide an engaging and controlled environment where patients can repeatedly practice cognitive tasks, reinforcing neuroplastic changes.

2. Emotional and behavioral recovery

TBI can also lead to emotional and behavioral difficulties, including mood swings, depression, and aggression. Neuroplasticity can support emotional recovery by helping the brain develop new ways of processing emotions and regulating behavior.

Psychotherapy and neuroplasticity: Cognitive-behavioral therapy (CBT) and other forms of psychotherapy can help patients rewire maladaptive thought patterns. Through repeated practice of new emotional regulation strategies, patients can reshape neural circuits to improve emotional control and behavior.

Factors influencing Neuroplastic recovery

Not all brain injury recoveries are the same, and several factors can influence the extent and speed of neuroplastic recovery. These factors include age, the severity of the injury, rehabilitation efforts, and environmental stimulation.

1. Age and Neuroplasticity

While neuroplasticity occurs throughout life, younger brains are typically more adaptable. Children and adolescents often experience more rapid and complete recoveries from brain injury than older adults due to higher levels of neurogenesis and synaptic plasticity. However, older individuals can still experience significant neuroplastic recovery with the right interventions.

2. Rehabilitation intensity

The intensity and duration of rehabilitation efforts significantly impact the brain's ability to recover through neuroplasticity. Consistent, focused therapy over long periods can promote more substantial neural changes.

Early intervention: Starting rehabilitation soon after the injury maximizes the brain's capacity for neuroplastic change, as the brain is most malleable during the early stages of recovery.

Long-term therapy: Neuroplastic changes continue to occur months or even years after the injury, meaning that long-term rehabilitation efforts can lead to continued improvements in function.

3. Environmental enrichment

The brain thrives in stimulating environments, which promote neuroplastic changes and support recovery. Patients recovering from brain injuries can benefit from exposure to novel and enriching experiences, such as engaging in new activities, social interaction, and learning new skills.

Occupational therapy: Engaging patients in meaningful, real-life activities through occupational therapy helps the brain adapt to challenges and reinforces neuroplastic changes.

Music therapy: Music therapy has been shown to stimulate brain regions involved in movement, emotion, and cognition, promoting neuroplastic recovery in a range of functions.

Future directions: Enhancing Neuroplasticity in Recovery

New technologies and treatments that enhance neuroplasticity offer promising avenues for improving recovery outcomes in patients with brain injuries.

1. Brain-Computer Interfaces (BCIs)

BCIs are devices that allow direct communication between the brain and external devices, such as computers or prosthetics. These technologies are being developed to help individuals with severe motor impairments regain function by bypassing damaged brain circuits and controlling movement through alternative pathways.

2. Pharmacological enhancers of Neuroplasticity

Researchers are exploring the use of drugs that can enhance neuroplasticity, such as those that increase levels of brain-derived neurotrophic factor (BDNF) or other neurotrophic factors. These drugs could potentially improve recovery outcomes by accelerating the brain's ability to form new connections.

3. Gene therapy

Gene therapy holds promise for enhancing neuroplasticity in individuals recovering from brain injuries. By modifying the expression of specific genes involved in neuroplastic processes, researchers hope to promote more efficient neural repair and recovery.

Chapter 8: Neuroplasticity across the Lifespan

Neuroplasticity, the brain's remarkable ability to reorganize itself by forming new neural connections, is a lifelong process. While it was once believed that the brain's capacity for change was limited to early development, research now shows that neuroplasticity persists from infancy through adulthood and into old age. However, the nature and degree of plasticity vary across different stages of life. Understanding these variations can offer insights into learning, memory, and even the potential for rehabilitation following injury or disease.

Infancy and early childhood: Rapid Plasticity

During the first few years of life, neuroplasticity is at its peak. This period is marked by an overproduction of synapses, the connections between neurons, which allows the brain to be highly adaptable to its environment. This phase of heightened plasticity is crucial for basic cognitive, sensory, and motor development.

- **Synaptic growth:** By age two or three, a child's brain has more than double the number of synapses an adult brain has. This overproduction allows for the rapid acquisition of language, motor skills, and emotional regulation. During this stage, children are highly receptive to learning from their surroundings, which is why early childhood education is so critical.
- **Pruning:** As the child grows, the brain begins to "prune" unused synaptic connections, refining and strengthening the neural pathways that are most frequently activated. This process makes the brain more efficient, but also highlights the importance of enriching environments and experiences during early childhood.

Adolescence: Reorganization and Sensitivity

Adolescence is another significant period of neuroplasticity. While the brain continues to prune excess connections, it also undergoes substantial reorganization, particularly in areas related to executive function, decision-making, and emotional regulation.

- **Prefrontal Cortex Development:** The prefrontal cortex, responsible for higher-order thinking and impulse control, matures throughout adolescence and into early adulthood. This is why teenagers can experience heightened emotional sensitivity and risk-taking behavior, as the brain is still developing the capacity for self-regulation.
- **Learning and Habits:** Adolescents are particularly receptive to acquiring new habits and skills. This phase is an optimal window for learning complex tasks, such as mastering a musical instrument or becoming proficient in a sport. However, it is also a time when maladaptive behaviors, like addiction, can take hold due to the brain's heightened plasticity.

Adulthood: Continued Learning and Adaptation

In adulthood, the brain's neuroplasticity may slow down compared to childhood, but it remains highly capable of forming new connections and reorganizing itself. Adult neuroplasticity is often more specific, driven by focused attention, learning, and adaptation to new experiences or challenges.

- **Learning New Skills:** Adults can continue to learn new languages, adapt to new technologies, or acquire complex skills throughout life. The process of learning actively engages neuroplasticity, reinforcing the idea that mental exercise is vital for maintaining brain health.
- **Cognitive Reserve:** Engaging in cognitively stimulating activities can help build what is known

as "cognitive reserve," resilience against cognitive decline. Activities such as reading, learning new hobbies, and social interaction can keep the brain adaptable and healthy.
- **Plasticity in Response to Injury:** Neuroplasticity plays a key role in recovery after brain injuries, such as strokes. In adulthood, the brain can "re-route" functions that were previously performed by damaged areas, often by recruiting nearby neurons to take over the lost function. While recovery may take longer compared to children, the brain retains a remarkable ability to heal and adapt.

Older Age: Adaptive Plasticity and Decline

Neuroplasticity continues into older age, though at a slower pace. While aging is associated with natural cognitive decline, the brain still maintains a degree of flexibility, particularly in response to learning and experience.

- **Neurogenesis:** Contrary to earlier beliefs, older adults can generate new neurons, particularly in the hippocampus, a region involved in memory. However, the rate of neurogenesis declines with age, contributing to slower learning and memory retrieval.
- **Use it or lose it:** Cognitive decline in old age is not inevitable. Older adults who remain mentally and physically active, maintain social connections, and engage in lifelong learning tend to experience slower rates of cognitive decline. Activities that challenge the brain, such as puzzles, reading, or learning new skills, can stimulate neuroplasticity, even in advanced age.
- **Rehabilitation and brain health:** Neuroplasticity in older adults is especially important for recovery from brain-related conditions like stroke or dementia. Rehabilitation programs that focus on relearning motor and cognitive skills leverage neuroplasticity to help

patients regain lost functions, though the recovery may be slower than in younger individuals.

Factors That Influence Neuroplasticity across the Lifespan

Several factors can impact the brain's ability to reorganize and form new connections throughout life. Some of the most significant include:

- **Environmental Enrichment:** Exposure to new experiences, education, and stimulation fosters neuroplasticity at any age. Enriched environments provide the brain with the input needed to create new neural pathways.
- **Physical Exercise:** Regular physical activity increases blood flow to the brain, promotes neurogenesis, and supports overall brain health. Exercise is particularly effective in promoting plasticity in the hippocampus, which is crucial for learning and memory.
- **Sleep:** Adequate sleep is essential for neuroplasticity, particularly in the consolidation of memories. Sleep deprivation impairs the brain's ability to form new connections, negatively affecting learning and memory.
- **Diet:** A balanced diet rich in antioxidants, omega-3 fatty acids, and essential nutrients supports brain health and neuroplasticity. Conversely, poor diet and obesity can hinder the brain's ability to adapt.
- **Stress and Mental Health:** Chronic stress can impair neuroplasticity, particularly in areas of the brain involved in memory and emotional regulation. Mindfulness practices, stress management, and mental health support are crucial for maintaining neuroplasticity across the lifespan.

Chapter 9: Neuroplasticity and Mental Health

The link between neuroplasticity and mental health is profound and increasingly recognized in the fields of psychiatry and psychology. While neuroplasticity enables the brain to adapt and change in response to experiences, learning, and recovery from injury, it also plays a significant role in the development, persistence, and treatment of mental health conditions.

In this chapter, we'll explore how neuroplasticity influences mental health, the neural mechanisms underlying mental health disorders, and how therapeutic interventions can harness neuroplasticity to improve emotional well-being.

The connection between Neuroplasticity and Mental Health

Mental health disorders often arise from maladaptive changes in the brain's neural circuits. Neuroplasticity, while essential for learning and recovery, can also result in the reinforcement of harmful behaviors and thought patterns. For instance, chronic stress or trauma can lead to negative neuroplastic changes that contribute to the development of anxiety, depression, or post-traumatic stress disorder (PTSD).

On the flip side, neuroplasticity also offers hope for mental health treatment. Many therapeutic approaches, including cognitive-behavioral therapy (CBT), mindfulness, and even medications, rely on the brain's ability to reorganize itself to foster positive, adaptive changes.

Neuroplasticity in anxiety and depression

1. Depression and the brain's rewiring

Depression is associated with structural and functional changes in key brain regions, including the prefrontal cortex, hippocampus, and amygdala. These changes can impair mood regulation, decision-making, and emotional processing, contributing to the characteristic symptoms of depression, such as persistent sadness, anhedonia (loss of pleasure), and cognitive difficulties.

Hippocampal shrinkage: Chronic depression can lead to a reduction in the size of the hippocampus, the brain region involved in memory and emotional regulation. This shrinkage is associated with impaired cognitive function and difficulty regulating emotions.

Reduced synaptic plasticity: In people with depression, there is often a reduction in synaptic plasticity—the ability of neurons to strengthen or weaken their connections based on activity. This impaired plasticity affects learning, memory, and the ability to adapt to new experiences.

Dysfunction in the prefrontal cortex: Depression often involves changes in the prefrontal cortex, which is responsible for executive functions like decision-making and self-regulation. Reduced activity in this region contributes to difficulty concentrating and making decisions.

However, neuroplasticity also plays a role in recovery from depression. Treatments that promote neuroplastic changes, such as antidepressant medications, electroconvulsive therapy (ECT), and cognitive therapy, can help reverse some of the brain changes associated with depression.

2. Anxiety Disorders and hyperactivity in fear circuits

Anxiety disorders, including generalized anxiety disorder (GAD), social anxiety, and panic disorder, involve heightened sensitivity and overactivity in the brain's fear circuits, particularly the amygdala. Neuroplastic changes in these circuits can make the brain more reactive to perceived threats, even in the absence of real danger.

Amygdala hyperactivity: The amygdala is central to processing fear and emotions. In individuals with anxiety, the amygdala becomes hyperactive, leading to heightened fear responses. Over time, this heightened reactivity becomes ingrained, creating a vicious cycle of anxiety.

Weakened regulation by the prefrontal cortex: Normally, the prefrontal cortex helps regulate emotional responses by downregulating the activity of the amygdala. In anxiety disorders, this regulatory pathway can become weakened, allowing the amygdala to dominate emotional responses.

Therapeutic interventions, such as CBT or exposure therapy, aim to reduce anxiety by altering these maladaptive neuroplastic changes. By repeatedly confronting feared situations in a safe context, individuals can weaken the connections between the fear response and the stimulus, promoting healthier patterns of brain activity.

The Impact of trauma and stress on Neuroplasticity

Chronic stress and trauma can profoundly affect neuroplasticity, often leading to maladaptive brain changes that underlie mental health conditions like PTSD, depression, and anxiety. The brain's stress response system, which involves the hypothalamus, pituitary gland, and adrenal glands (the HPA axis), plays a key role in these changes.

Stress and hippocampal atrophy: Prolonged exposure to stress hormones, particularly cortisol, can cause atrophy in the hippocampus. This contributes to memory difficulties and impairs the brain's ability to regulate emotions.

Strengthening of fear circuits: Trauma can strengthen the connections between the amygdala and other brain regions, creating hyperactive fear circuits that remain overactive even after the trauma has passed. This underlies the hypervigilance, flashbacks, and exaggerated startle responses seen in PTSD.

Disruption of prefrontal regulation: Chronic stress disrupts the functioning of the prefrontal cortex, reducing its ability to regulate emotional responses and make decisions.

While these changes can be debilitating, neuroplasticity also allows for recovery from trauma. Therapeutic interventions such as eye movement desensitization and reprocessing (EMDR), trauma-focused CBT, and mindfulness practices can help retrain the brain to reduce the intensity of traumatic memories and restore emotional balance.

Harnessing Neuroplasticity for mental health treatment

One of the most promising aspects of neuroplasticity is its role in mental health treatments. Through various therapeutic interventions, the brain can be trained to form new, healthier neural connections that promote emotional well-being. Below are some key approaches that leverage neuroplasticity in mental health treatment.

1. Cognitive Behavioral Therapy (CBT)

CBT is a widely used and effective treatment for anxiety, depression, and other mental health disorders. It works by helping individuals identify and challenge negative thought patterns and behaviors that contribute to their symptoms. By doing so, CBT promotes positive neuroplastic changes in the brain, particularly in areas involved in emotional regulation and executive function.

Strengthening prefrontal cortex activity: CBT helps strengthen the prefrontal cortex's ability to regulate emotions, improving an individual's capacity to manage stress and control impulsive reactions.

Weakening negative thought patterns: By repeatedly challenging negative beliefs and replacing them with more positive or realistic ones, CBT helps weaken the neural circuits that support maladaptive thoughts.

Through regular CBT sessions, individuals can gradually rewire their brains to reduce anxiety, improve mood, and enhance coping mechanisms.

2. Mindfulness and Meditation

Mindfulness and meditation practices have been shown to promote positive neuroplastic changes, particularly in regions of the brain associated with attention, emotional regulation, and stress reduction. Mindfulness meditation encourages individuals to focus on the present moment, reducing rumination and improving their ability to manage negative emotions.

Increased gray matter in the prefrontal cortex: Regular meditation has been associated with increased gray matter volume in the prefrontal cortex, which enhances emotional regulation, attention, and decision-making.

Reduced amygdala reactivity: Studies show that mindfulness meditation can reduce activity in the amygdala, decreasing the brain's reactivity to stress and emotional triggers.

By promoting neuroplasticity, mindfulness helps individuals build resilience to stress and improve mental health outcomes.

3. Antidepressant and Psychotropic m

Certain medications used to treat mental health disorders also promote neuroplastic changes in the brain. For example:

Selective Serotonin Reuptake Inhibitors (SSRIs), commonly prescribed for depression and anxiety, increase the availability of serotonin in the brain, which promotes synaptic plasticity. SSRIs also encourage neurogenesis in the hippocampus, potentially reversing the effects of depression-related hippocampal shrinkage.

Ketamine, a relatively new treatment for depression, has been found to promote rapid synaptogenesis and enhance connectivity in brain regions involved in mood regulation. Its fast-acting neuroplastic effects make it a promising treatment for severe depression.

Medications that promote neuroplasticity are often used in combination with therapy to maximize their effects.

4. Physical Exercise

Physical exercise has long been known to have mental health benefits, and its effects on neuroplasticity provide insight into why it's such a powerful tool for emotional well-being.

Increased production of BDNF: Exercise stimulates the release of brain-derived neurotrophic factor (BDNF), which supports the growth, maintenance, and survival of neurons. BDNF also promotes synaptic plasticity, helping the brain adapt to new learning and experiences.

Improved hippocampal function: Regular physical activity can increase the size of the hippocampus, helping to improve memory and emotional regulation. This is particularly important in reducing symptoms of depression and anxiety.

Exercise-based interventions are often incorporated into mental health treatment plans to harness their neuroplastic benefits.

Neuroplasticity in addiction recovery

Addiction is another area where neuroplasticity plays a crucial role. Substance use disorders are characterized by the brain's maladaptive plastic changes in response to repeated drug use. These changes can strengthen reward pathways and weaken self-regulation, making it difficult to break the cycle of addiction.

Rewiring reward circuits: Drugs of abuse can hijack the brain's reward system by releasing large amounts of dopamine, which strengthens the neural pathways associated with cravings and compulsive behavior. Over time, this leads to long-lasting changes in brain structure and function, reinforcing the addiction.

Restoring balance through neuroplasticity: Recovery from addiction involves rewiring the brain's reward circuits and restoring balance to the prefrontal cortex, which governs decision-making and impulse control. Behavioral therapies, such as contingency management and cognitive-behavioral approaches, help weaken the neural connections that drive addictive behaviors.

Future Directions: Neuroplasticity and novel mental health treatments

Research on neuroplasticity has led to the development of new treatments that directly target the brain's ability to change. These innovative approaches aim to harness neuroplasticity in ways that go beyond traditional therapy and medication.

1. Transcranial Magnetic Stimulation (TMS)

TMS is a non-invasive procedure that uses magnetic fields to stimulate nerve cells in specific areas of the brain, particularly the prefrontal cortex. It has been shown to improve neuroplasticity in patients with depression and other mental health disorders by:

Enhancing synaptic plasticity: TMS increases the excitability of neurons, making it easier for new neural connections to form and strengthening existing ones.

Targeting underactive brain regions: By stimulating the prefrontal cortex, TMS can improve mood regulation and cognitive function, helping alleviate symptoms of depression and anxiety.

2. Psychedelic-Assisted Therapy

Psychedelics such as psilocybin, LSD, and MDMA are being explored for their potential to promote neuroplasticity and enhance mental health outcomes. When used in a controlled therapeutic setting, these substances may:

Promote synaptogenesis: Psychedelics have been shown to stimulate the growth of new synapses, particularly in the prefrontal cortex, which could help reverse some of the neural deficits seen in depression and PTSD.

Facilitate emotional breakthroughs: Psychedelics may help patients access repressed emotions or memories, allowing for profound therapeutic insights and fostering more adaptive neural connections.

3. Neurofeedback

Neurofeedback is a technique that trains individuals to regulate their brain activity by providing real-time feedback on brainwave patterns. By promoting awareness and control of brain activity, neurofeedback can help reshape neural circuits associated with mental health disorders, including anxiety, ADHD, and PTSD.

Modifying brainwave patterns: Through neurofeedback, individuals can learn to modify maladaptive brainwave patterns and reinforce more stable, balanced activity. This can promote greater emotional regulation and cognitive clarity.

Chapter 10: Neuroplasticity and Learning

Neuroplasticity is at the heart of how we learn. From acquiring new skills to mastering languages, the brain's ability to form, strengthen, and reorganize neural connections is fundamental to the learning process. Whether it's the education of young children, skill development in adulthood, or rehabilitation after injury, neuroplasticity enables the brain to adapt and grow throughout life.

In this chapter, we'll explore how neuroplasticity influences learning, the stages of neuroplastic change, and techniques to enhance the brain's capacity for learning.

The Brain's Learning Process: Neuroplasticity in Action

Learning involves the formation of new neural connections and the modification of existing ones. Each time we encounter new information or practice a skill, neurons in our brain fire and create or strengthen synaptic connections. The more we engage in this learning process, the stronger and more efficient these neural circuits become.

1. Synaptic Plasticity and Learning

Synaptic plasticity refers to the ability of synapses—the connections between neurons—to change in strength. This is the fundamental mechanism underlying learning and memory. Two key forms of synaptic plasticity play important roles in the learning process:

Long-Term Potentiation (LTP): LTP is the strengthening of synaptic connections as a result of repeated stimulation. When neurons are frequently activated together, the connection between them becomes stronger, making it easier for them to fire in the future. This process is critical for long-term memory formation and skill acquisition.

Long-Term Depression (LTD): LTD is the weakening of synaptic connections when they are used less frequently. This process allows the brain to discard irrelevant or outdated information, making room for new learning. LTD helps ensure that the brain remains efficient and adaptable by pruning unnecessary connections.

The balance between LTP and LTD allows the brain to optimize its learning capacity, strengthening valuable information while discarding what is no longer needed.

2. Structural Plasticity and the Formation of New Connections

In addition to strengthening existing connections, learning can lead to structural plasticity, where the brain forms entirely new synaptic connections or even new neurons in some cases. This type of plasticity is particularly important when learning complex or novel tasks, as the brain may need to rewire itself to accommodate new patterns of thought or behavior.

Synaptogenesis: The process of forming new synapses allows for the development of new neural pathways. For example, when learning to play a musical instrument, the brain creates new connections to control fine motor skills, auditory processing, and memory simultaneously.

Neurogenesis: While once thought to occur only in early development, research shows that neurogenesis—the birth of new neurons—continues into adulthood, particularly in the hippocampus, a region involved in learning and memory. Activities like physical exercise and mental stimulation promote neurogenesis, enhancing the brain's capacity to learn.

Stages of Neuroplasticity in Learning

Learning through neuroplasticity typically unfolds in three stages: acquisition, consolidation, and retention.

1. Acquisition

During the acquisition phase, the brain is exposed to new information or experiences. At this stage, neuroplastic changes begin to take place as the brain forms new synaptic connections and strengthens existing ones.

Short-term memory: Initially, new information is stored in short-term memory. Neuroplastic changes during this stage are still fragile, and without reinforcement, the new connections may weaken or disappear.

Practice and repetition: To transition information from short-term to long-term memory, repeated practice is essential. The more a person engages with the material or skill, the stronger the synaptic connections become, solidifying the learning process.

2. Consolidation

The consolidation phase is when newly acquired information becomes more stable in long-term memory. This process often occurs during rest or sleep, allowing the brain to reinforce and reorganize neural connections. Key factors involved in consolidation include:

Sleep: Sleep is crucial for neuroplasticity, particularly the consolidation of memories. During sleep, the brain replays experiences from the day, strengthening neural pathways and allowing new information to become more deeply ingrained.

Rest: Periods of rest or downtime during the learning process allow the brain to consolidate information. Research shows that the brain continues to process information even when not actively engaged in learning, making rest an important part of memory consolidation.

3. Retention

In the retention stage, the brain maintains and refines the learned information over time. Strong neural circuits formed during the acquisition and consolidation phases become more permanent, allowing for the retention of skills or knowledge.

Active recall: Engaging in activities that require recalling learned information, such as testing or teaching others, helps reinforce neural pathways, making memories more accessible in the future.

Spaced repetition: Repeating learned material at intervals, rather than cramming, is a highly effective way to improve retention. Spaced repetition capitalizes on neuroplasticity by revisiting the information at just the right time to strengthen connections.

Enhancing Learning Through Neuroplasticity

There are several strategies to enhance learning by tapping into the brain's natural capacity for neuroplasticity. These techniques are particularly useful for students, professionals, and anyone seeking to learn more efficiently and retain knowledge over the long term.

1. Repetition and Practice

Repetition is a fundamental principle of learning, driving the synaptic changes necessary for mastering skills or retaining knowledge. When repeated practice is spaced out over time, it leads to stronger, more durable neural connections.

Deliberate practice: Focusing on specific areas of improvement and gradually increasing difficulty during practice sessions helps the brain adapt and form stronger connections. Deliberate practice is more effective than passive repetition because it actively engages the brain's problem-solving and adaptive capacities.

2. Multisensory Learning

Engaging multiple senses during the learning process can enhance neuroplasticity by activating different parts of the brain simultaneously. For example, combining visual, auditory, and kinesthetic learning strategies leads to more robust neural connections, as different sensory modalities reinforce each other.

Examples of multisensory learning: Reading aloud (visual and auditory), using tactile objects to teach mathematical concepts (kinesthetic and visual), or learning a language through speaking, listening, and writing.

3. Active Engagement and Curiosity

Learning is more effective when the brain is actively engaged and curious. Activities that stimulate curiosity and problem-solving lead to stronger neuroplastic changes because they activate higher-order cognitive processes.

Problem-based learning: Encouraging learners to solve complex, real-world problems engages the brain in meaningful ways, promoting deeper understanding and better retention of material.

Self-directed learning: When individuals take charge of their own learning, exploring topics of personal interest or applying knowledge in creative ways, they strengthen their brain's ability to learn independently.

4. Rest and Sleep for Consolidation

As discussed, sleep and rest are vital for memory consolidation. Ensuring adequate sleep and taking breaks during study sessions allow the brain to process and reinforce new information.

Sleep hygiene: Maintaining good sleep habits, such as sticking to a consistent sleep schedule and creating a restful environment, supports neuroplasticity and learning.

Naps: Short naps, particularly following periods of intense learning, can enhance memory consolidation and improve recall.

5. Physical Exercise and Neuroplasticity

Physical exercise promotes neuroplasticity by stimulating the release of growth factors like brain-derived neurotrophic factor (BDNF), which supports the growth of new neurons and synapses. Exercise also enhances blood flow to the brain, improving cognitive function.

Aerobic exercise: Activities like running, swimming, or cycling have been shown to increase BDNF levels and improve memory and learning capacity.

Exercise breaks: Incorporating short bursts of physical activity during study sessions can help refresh the brain and enhance learning.

6. Technology and Neuroplasticity

Advancements in technology provide new tools to enhance neuroplasticity and learning. Educational apps, virtual reality, and neurofeedback are just a few examples of how technology can engage the brain in ways that promote efficient learning.

Educational apps and gamification: Interactive apps that use gamification principles to teach skills or knowledge activate reward circuits in the brain, making learning more engaging and effective.

Neurofeedback: By providing real-time feedback on brainwave activity, neurofeedback can help individuals optimize their brain function during learning. This technology is particularly useful for enhancing focus and concentration.

Neuroplasticity and Lifelong Learning

The idea that neuroplasticity diminishes with age has been challenged by recent research showing that the brain remains capable of learning and adapting throughout life. Lifelong learning not only keeps the brain sharp but also promotes ongoing neuroplasticity, protecting against cognitive decline and enhancing quality of life.

1. Learning in Adulthood and Old Age

While learning in adulthood may require more effort compared to early childhood, adults can still develop new skills and knowledge through neuroplastic processes. Factors that promote lifelong learning include:

Cognitive challenges: Continuously engaging in cognitively demanding activities, such as learning a new language, playing a musical instrument, or solving puzzles, promotes neuroplasticity in adulthood.

Social interaction: Engaging in meaningful social activities stimulates neuroplasticity by requiring the brain to navigate complex social environments, process emotions, and solve problems.

Lifelong hobbies and skills: Pursuing hobbies such as painting, playing a musical instrument, or learning a new sport fosters continual engagement with novel challenges, which stimulates neuroplasticity. These activities keep the brain adaptable and open to forming new neural connections, even in later stages of life.

Neuroplasticity in Education

Neuroplasticity has significant implications for educational practices. Understanding how the brain learns can inform more effective teaching strategies that align with the brain's natural processes of acquiring and retaining information.

1. Personalized Learning and Neuroplasticity

Every individual's brain is different, and personalized learning approaches that take into account different learning styles and paces can better engage neuroplastic processes. Tailoring instruction to the needs of the learner allows for:

Targeted skill development: Providing students with customized learning paths that address their strengths and weaknesses promotes more efficient learning by focusing on areas where neuroplastic changes are most needed.

Adapting instruction to brain development: Recognizing that brain development occurs at different rates in individuals, particularly during adolescence, allows educators to design curricula that align with these developmental stages, maximizing the brain's learning potential.

2. Growth Mindset and Neuroplasticity

A growth mindset, the belief that abilities and intelligence can be developed through effort and learning, is closely tied to the concept of neuroplasticity. By fostering a growth mindset in students, educators can encourage them to embrace challenges and persist in the face of difficulties, knowing that their brains can adapt and grow through hard work and practice.

Shifting beliefs: Teaching students about neuroplasticity can help them understand that failure is a natural part of learning and that the brain's ability to change means they can improve over time. This reduces fear of failure and promotes resilience.

Encouraging effort and practice: The more students believe that effort leads to improvement, the more likely they are to engage in activities that promote neuroplasticity, such as repeated practice and trying out new learning strategies.

Chapter 11: Harnessing Neuroplasticity with age progression

As we age, cognitive abilities such as memory, attention, and processing speed tend to decline. However, the concept of neuroplasticity offers a hopeful perspective on the aging brain. Despite the natural slowing of certain cognitive processes, the brain remains adaptable throughout life, capable of forming new neural connections and strengthening existing ones. Aging does not have to be synonymous with cognitive decline—through neuroplasticity, individuals can retain mental sharpness, adapt to new challenges, and even continue learning well into their later years.

In this chapter, we'll explore how neuroplasticity operates in the aging brain, factors that influence cognitive resilience, and strategies to maintain and enhance neuroplasticity as we grow older.

How Neuroplasticity changes with age

While neuroplasticity persists throughout life, the brain undergoes structural and functional changes with age that can influence its capacity for adaptability. Understanding these changes can help us identify ways to support neuroplasticity in older adults.

1. Structural changes in the aging brain

Neuron loss: While significant neuron loss is not as prevalent as once believed, the brain does experience some reduction in neuron density as we age. This can affect the ability to form new connections, but the brain compensates by making more efficient use of existing pathways.

Synaptic decline: The number of synapses, or connections between neurons, decreases with age. This can slow down communication between different parts of the brain, which affects processing speed and memory.

Myelin degradation: Myelin, the protective sheath that insulates nerve fibers and speeds up neural communication, tends to degrade over time. This results in slower transmission of signals between neurons, which may contribute to slower cognitive processing in older adults.

2. Functional changes and Neuroplasticity

Despite these structural changes, the brain maintains the capacity for functional neuroplasticity. Older brains can still learn new skills, adapt to changes, and recover from damage, although the process may take longer compared to younger brains.

Compensatory mechanisms: The aging brain often engages compensatory strategies to make up for lost or weakened functions. For example, older adults may rely on both hemispheres of the brain for tasks that younger adults complete using only one hemisphere. This kind of compensation supports ongoing functionality and cognitive resilience.

Cognitive reserve: Cognitive reserve refers to the brain's ability to cope with damage or age-related decline by utilizing alternative neural pathways. Individuals with higher cognitive reserve, often developed through education, lifelong learning, and mentally stimulating activities, are more resilient to cognitive decline.

Neuroplasticity and cognitive Health in aging

Neuroplasticity is central to maintaining cognitive health as we age. Engaging in activities that challenge the brain can promote neuroplasticity, helping to preserve memory, attention, and problem-solving skills. The concept of "use it or lose it" is particularly relevant to the aging brain.

1. Memory and Neuroplasticity

Memory decline is one of the most common concerns associated with aging, but neuroplasticity offers ways to mitigate this decline.

Hippocampal neurogenesis: The hippocampus, a region involved in forming new memories, remains capable of generating new neurons throughout life, a process known as neurogenesis. Physical exercise, mental stimulation, and even certain dietary factors can enhance neurogenesis, supporting memory retention.

Memory strategies: Older adults can use memory aids, mnemonic devices, and repetition to reinforce neuroplastic changes and improve memory function. Repeated exposure to information strengthens synaptic connections, making it easier to recall memories.

2. Attention and Processing Speed

Attention and processing speed often decline with age, making it harder to focus on tasks or quickly process information. However, neuroplasticity allows the brain to adapt by improving attention through targeted activities.

Mindfulness and attention training: Mindfulness meditation and attention-training exercises have been shown to improve focus and cognitive flexibility in older adults. By regularly practicing these techniques, individuals can enhance their ability to concentrate and slow cognitive decline related to attention.

Cognitive exercises: Activities that challenge attention, such as puzzles, memory games, and brain-training apps, can promote neuroplasticity by keeping the brain engaged and responsive to new information.

3. Emotional regulation and Neuroplasticity

Emotional regulation tends to improve with age, with many older adults experiencing greater emotional stability compared to younger individuals. Neuroplasticity supports this process by enabling the brain to adapt to emotional experiences and develop healthier coping mechanisms.

Cognitive-behavioral strategies: Older adults can use cognitive-behavioral techniques, such as reframing negative thoughts and practicing gratitude, to strengthen neural circuits associated with emotional control. Over time, these practices can reinforce the brain's capacity to manage emotions effectively.

Factors that enhance Neuroplasticity in aging

Several lifestyle factors can influence neuroplasticity in aging, contributing to cognitive health and resilience. By adopting certain habits, individuals can promote brain plasticity and reduce the risk of cognitive decline.

1. Physical Exercise

Exercise is one of the most powerful stimulants of neuroplasticity, particularly in the aging brain. Regular physical activity promotes the release of brain-derived neurotrophic factor (BDNF), a protein that supports the growth of new neurons and synaptic connections.

Aerobic exercise: Activities such as walking, swimming, and cycling are particularly beneficial for cognitive health. Aerobic exercise increases blood flow to the brain, stimulates neurogenesis in the hippocampus, and enhances overall brain function.

Strength training: In addition to aerobic activities, strength training can also improve cognitive function. Studies show that resistance exercises help enhance memory and executive functions by promoting neuroplastic changes in the brain.

2. Mental Stimulation

Engaging in mentally stimulating activities is crucial for maintaining neuroplasticity in older adults. Lifelong learning and cognitive challenges can help keep the brain flexible and adaptable.

Learning new skills: Learning a new language, musical instrument, or even a new hobby promotes the formation of new neural connections. Challenging the brain with novel tasks encourages neuroplasticity by requiring it to adapt to unfamiliar information.

Puzzles and games: Activities like crossword puzzles, Sudoku, and strategy games provide mental stimulation that keeps the brain engaged. These activities challenge cognitive abilities such as memory, attention, and problem-solving, promoting neuroplasticity.

3. Social engagement

Social interaction plays a vital role in maintaining neuroplasticity in aging. Engaging with others stimulates various cognitive and emotional processes, keeping the brain active and resilient.

Social activities: Participation in social clubs, group activities, or even regular conversations with friends and family can enhance cognitive function. Social interactions require the brain to process emotions, language, and complex social cues, all of which promote neuroplasticity.

Volunteering: Many older adults find fulfillment in volunteering, which not only offers social engagement but also provides a sense of purpose. This combination of cognitive and emotional stimulation is beneficial for neuroplasticity.

4. Nutrition and brain health

Diet also influences neuroplasticity, particularly in aging. Certain nutrients have been shown to support brain health by promoting neurogenesis, reducing inflammation, and protecting against cognitive decline.

Antioxidant-rich foods: Foods high in antioxidants, such as fruits, vegetables, and nuts, help protect the brain from oxidative stress, which can damage neurons and inhibit neuroplasticity.

Omega-3 fatty acids: Found in fish like salmon and flaxseeds, omega-3 fatty acids support the integrity of neuronal membranes and promote synaptic plasticity. These nutrients are particularly beneficial for preserving cognitive function in older adults.

Anti-inflammatory foods: Chronic inflammation can impair neuroplasticity and contribute to cognitive decline. Incorporating anti-inflammatory foods like leafy greens, turmeric, and berries into the diet can reduce inflammation and support brain health.

Neuroplasticity and cognitive decline: Dementia and Alzheimer's Disease

Neuroplasticity offers hope for mitigating some aspects of age-related cognitive decline, including dementia and Alzheimer's disease. While these conditions are progressive, promoting neuroplasticity through lifestyle interventions may help delay their onset or slow their progression.

1. Delaying cognitive decline

Cognitive reserve: Individuals with higher cognitive reserve are often able to delay the onset of dementia symptoms, even when the underlying pathology (such as amyloid plaques) is present. Lifelong learning, social engagement, and mental stimulation all contribute to building cognitive reserve, which supports neuroplasticity in the face of neurodegenerative conditions.

2. Early Intervention

Early intervention is key to preserving neuroplasticity in individuals diagnosed with mild cognitive impairment (MCI) or early-stage dementia. Cognitive training, physical exercise, and other neuroplasticity-enhancing activities can help slow cognitive decline and improve quality of life.

Strategies for promoting Neuroplasticity in aging

By implementing certain practices, older adults can actively promote neuroplasticity and maintain cognitive health.

1. Lifelong learning

Continued education, whether through formal classes or self-directed learning, keeps the brain engaged and adaptive. Learning something new challenges the brain to form new connections, supporting neuroplasticity well into old age.

2. Regular physical activity

Exercise remains one of the most effective ways to support neuroplasticity. Engaging in both aerobic and strength-training exercises several times a week can enhance cognitive function and reduce the risk of cognitive decline.

3. Social connection

Maintaining strong social ties and engaging in meaningful social activities helps stimulate cognitive and emotional processes that support neuroplasticity.

4. Cognitive challenges

Puzzles, brain games, and strategy-based activities keep the brain active and promote neuroplasticity by engaging problem-solving and memory skills.

5. Balanced diet and Neuroplasticity in aging

A balanced diet plays a crucial role in supporting neuroplasticity, especially as we age. The right nutrients can help maintain brain health, promote the formation of new neural connections, and protect against cognitive decline. Certain foods and nutrients have been shown to enhance cognitive function by reducing inflammation, increasing neurogenesis, and protecting neurons from damage.

Key Nutrients for Neuroplasticity

1. Omega-3 Fatty Acids

Omega-3 fatty acids, particularly docosahexaenoic acid (DHA) and eicosapentaenoic acid (EPA), are essential for brain health. These fatty acids are important for maintaining the structure of neuronal membranes and promoting synaptic plasticity.

Sources: Fatty fish like salmon, mackerel, sardines, flaxseeds, chia seeds, walnuts, and algae-based supplements.

Benefits: Omega-3s support neurogenesis, reduce neuroinflammation, and have been shown to improve memory, cognitive function, and mood in older adults.

2. Antioxidants

Antioxidants protect the brain from oxidative stress, a process that can damage neurons and impede neuroplasticity. By neutralizing free radicals, antioxidants help prevent the decline of cognitive function that comes with aging.

Sources: Berries (such as blueberries, strawberries, and blackberries), dark chocolate, nuts, seeds, spinach, kale, and green tea.

Benefits: Regular consumption of antioxidant-rich foods has been linked to better memory, improved learning, and a lower risk of developing age-related neurodegenerative diseases.

3. B Vitamins

B vitamins, particularly B6, B12, and folate (B9), play a key role in maintaining brain health by supporting the production of neurotransmitters and reducing levels of homocysteine, an amino acid associated with cognitive decline.

Sources: Leafy green vegetables, beans, whole grains, poultry, fish, eggs, and fortified cereals.

Benefits: Adequate levels of B vitamins are essential for cognitive function, mood regulation, and the prevention of age-related mental decline.

4. Polyphenols

Polyphenols are plant compounds that offer protective benefits for the brain. They promote neurogenesis, enhance synaptic plasticity, and reduce inflammation.

Sources: Green tea, red wine, dark chocolate, coffee, and colorful fruits and vegetables like grapes, apples, and onions.

Benefits: Polyphenols have been shown to improve memory and protect against cognitive decline by enhancing neuroplasticity and reducing inflammation.

5. Vitamin D

Vitamin D is important for overall brain health, as it supports cognitive function, reduces inflammation, and may enhance neuroplasticity by promoting the release of neurotrophic factors like BDNF.

Sources: Sunlight exposure, fortified foods (such as dairy products and cereals), fatty fish, and egg yolks.

Benefits: Low levels of vitamin D are linked to cognitive decline, so maintaining adequate levels can help preserve memory and cognitive function in older adults.

Anti-inflammatory foods

Chronic inflammation in the brain is linked to neurodegenerative diseases like Alzheimer's and Parkinson's. Consuming anti-inflammatory foods helps protect the brain from damage and supports neuroplasticity.

Sources: Turmeric (with curcumin), leafy greens, tomatoes, olive oil, fatty fish, and nuts.

Benefits: These foods help reduce neuroinflammation, supporting better memory, learning, and overall cognitive health.

Hydration and brain function

Dehydration can impair cognitive function, especially in older adults. Staying hydrated is essential for maintaining brain performance and supporting neuroplasticity.

Sources: Water, herbal teas, and hydrating foods like fruits and vegetables.

Benefits: Proper hydration ensures optimal brain function, improves attention and memory, and supports the brain's capacity for learning and adaptation.

The Mediterranean diet: A model for cognitive health

The Mediterranean diet, rich in vegetables, fruits, whole grains, legumes, olive oil, and fish, has been consistently associated with better cognitive function and a reduced risk of neurodegenerative diseases. This diet supports neuroplasticity through its focus on anti-inflammatory and antioxidant-rich foods.

Benefits: Studies suggest that adherence to the Mediterranean diet may slow age-related cognitive decline and protect against Alzheimer's disease.

Chapter 12: Neuroplasticity in the Age of Technology

The rise of technology has brought about profound changes in our daily lives, transforming the way we communicate, learn, work, and even think. As our interactions with technology increase, so does its influence on our brains. In the context of neuroplasticity, technology offers both challenges and opportunities. This chapter will explore how digital tools, devices, and platforms are shaping brain function, and how they can be leveraged to enhance neuroplasticity for learning, rehabilitation, and overall cognitive well-being.

The Impact of technology on Neuroplasticity

Technology has introduced a new environment in which our brains must adapt and evolve. Whether it's through constant exposure to digital devices, social media, video games, or online learning platforms, technology interacts with our brain's neuroplastic mechanisms. However, this interaction can have both positive and negative effects on the brain's ability to adapt, depending on how technology is used.

1. Digital distraction and attention span

One of the most discussed concerns about technology's influence on neuroplasticity is its potential to fragment attention. The constant stream of notifications, quick information access, and multitasking habits created by digital environments can condition the brain to operate in a state of divided attention.

Impact on attention: Frequent use of digital devices has been associated with shorter attention spans and a reduced ability to focus on complex, sustained tasks. The brain adapts to these rapid shifts in focus, weakening the neural circuits involved in deep concentration and long-term attention.

Neural rewiring: Multitasking with technology encourages the brain to wire itself for quick task-switching, rather than sustained focus. Over time, this can impact areas of the brain responsible for concentration, memory consolidation, and critical thinking.

2. Screen time and cognitive function

Extended periods of screen time, especially in children and adolescents, have raised concerns about the long-term impact on brain development. Excessive screen use can affect the brain's plasticity in ways that alter cognitive processes, including learning, memory, and emotional regulation.

Impact on brain development: Studies suggest that children who spend excessive time using screens may experience changes in the development of brain regions associated with executive function, language, and social skills. The brain adapts to digital stimuli, potentially at the expense of developing deeper cognitive skills.

Digital learning: While screen time has potential downsides, structured and interactive digital learning tools can enhance cognitive functions by promoting neuroplastic changes in brain areas related to problem-solving, memory, and analytical thinking.

3. Social media and emotional Neuroplasticity

Social media platforms, designed to capture attention and encourage engagement, influence not only cognitive processes but also emotional regulation. The brain's reward pathways, particularly the dopamine system, are highly sensitive to the intermittent reinforcement of likes, comments, and shares.

Reward circuitry: The use of social media can hijack the brain's reward systems by providing quick bursts of dopamine in response to notifications or interactions. Over time, this can alter the brain's reward circuitry, leading to addictive behaviors and reduced capacity for delayed gratification.

Emotional plasticity: Constant engagement with social media can also influence emotional neuroplasticity, shaping how the brain processes emotions like happiness, sadness, or anxiety. For example, negative feedback or comparison on social platforms can condition the brain to react with heightened stress or lower self-esteem, which may lead to altered emotional responses.

Leveraging technology to enhance Neuroplasticity

While there are concerns about the potential negative impacts of technology on neuroplasticity, there are also significant opportunities for technology to enhance brain function. Numerous digital tools and platforms are designed to promote neuroplasticity, particularly in areas of learning, cognitive rehabilitation, and brain training.

1. Brain training apps and cognitive enhancement

Digital brain training apps, such as Lumosity, Peak, and Elevate, have gained popularity for their ability to enhance cognitive function through structured exercises. These apps use gamified tasks to stimulate neuroplasticity in areas such as memory, attention, problem-solving, and reasoning.

Neuroplastic benefits: Regular use of brain training apps can lead to improved cognitive function by challenging the brain with novel tasks. The repeated practice encourages the formation of new synaptic connections, strengthening the neural circuits involved in cognitive processes.

Transfer effects: While some studies have shown improvements in the specific tasks practiced within brain training apps, there is ongoing debate about whether these skills transfer to real-world cognitive tasks. However, there is evidence to suggest that structured brain training can enhance overall brain health, particularly in older adults.

2. Virtual Reality (VR) and Neuroplasticity

Virtual reality is emerging as a powerful tool for promoting neuroplasticity, particularly in the fields of rehabilitation and therapy. VR environments create immersive, multisensory experiences that can be tailored to stimulate specific brain functions.

Rehabilitation: In stroke recovery and motor rehabilitation, VR allows patients to engage in task-specific activities that mimic real-world movements. By practicing these tasks in a virtual environment, the brain rewires itself to improve motor control and coordination.

Cognitive therapy: VR is also being used in cognitive therapy to treat conditions such as post-traumatic stress disorder (PTSD) and anxiety. By recreating controlled environments that trigger specific emotional responses, therapists can guide patients through desensitization exercises that promote neuroplastic changes in emotional processing circuits.

3. Neurofeedback and Brain-Computer Interfaces

Neurofeedback is a form of biofeedback that allows individuals to monitor their brain activity in real-time, using EEG (electroencephalogram) technology. By providing feedback about brainwave patterns, neurofeedback enables individuals to consciously regulate their brain activity, promoting neuroplasticity in specific regions of the brain.

Cognitive regulation: Neurofeedback has been used to enhance attention, focus, and emotional regulation by training individuals to modify their brainwave patterns. This can lead to improvements in cognitive function and emotional control, particularly in individuals with ADHD, anxiety, or depression.

Brain-computer interfaces (BCIs): BCIs are emerging technologies that allow direct communication between the brain and external devices. BCIs have shown promise in helping individuals with motor impairments regain control of movement by harnessing the brain's neuroplastic potential. For example, patients with paralysis can use BCIs to control robotic limbs or computer interfaces through thought alone, encouraging neuroplastic changes in motor circuits.

4. Online learning and cognitive growth

Online education platforms such as Coursera, edX, and Khan Academy offer vast opportunities for continuous learning. Engaging in lifelong learning, particularly in new and challenging subjects, promotes neuroplasticity by encouraging the brain to form new connections and strengthen existing ones.

Learning new skills: Learning new subjects, such as a language, musical instrument, or coding, stimulates neurogenesis and enhances synaptic plasticity. Online learning provides a convenient platform for individuals to engage in these cognitive challenges at any age.

Adaptive learning platforms: Some online learning platforms use adaptive algorithms to tailor the learning experience to the individual's pace and ability. These platforms optimize neuroplasticity by providing personalized challenges that target the learner's cognitive strengths and weaknesses.

Technology and Neuroplasticity across the lifespan

As technology continues to evolve, its impact on neuroplasticity will vary across different stages of life. The brain's ability to adapt to technological changes depends on age, cognitive health, and the way technology is integrated into daily activities.

1. Children and adolescents

For children and adolescents, technology is a double-edged sword. While educational apps, games, and online learning can stimulate cognitive growth and plasticity, excessive screen time or exposure to certain types of content (e.g., violent video games) can negatively affect brain development.

Guided use of technology: Parents and educators play a crucial role in guiding children's use of technology to ensure that it promotes healthy brain development. Encouraging the use of educational apps, limiting screen time, and balancing digital activities with physical and social interactions can foster positive neuroplasticity.

2. Adults

In adults, technology can be harnessed to maintain and enhance cognitive function. Digital platforms that encourage lifelong learning, brain training, or physical exercise can promote neuroplasticity, preventing cognitive decline associated with aging.

Cognitive maintenance: Engaging in mentally stimulating activities through technology, such as learning new skills or playing brain games, helps adults keep their brains sharp and adaptable. Additionally, technologies like VR can offer new ways to stay physically and cognitively active.

3. Older adults

For older adults, technology offers significant opportunities to slow age-related cognitive decline. Tools like brain training apps, online courses, and social media can keep the brain active, encouraging neuroplasticity even in later life.

Neuroplastic potential: While neuroplasticity declines with age, older adults can still form new neural connections through mentally and socially stimulating activities. Using technology to stay connected, learn new skills, and engage in physical exercise can enhance cognitive health and prolong independence.

Chapter 13: The Future of Neuroplasticity

As our understanding of neuroplasticity continues to evolve, so too does our ability to harness it for various applications in medicine, education, mental health, and even artificial intelligence. The future of neuroplasticity holds immense promise as research delves deeper into the mechanisms behind brain plasticity and as new technologies are developed to manipulate and enhance these mechanisms. In this chapter, we will explore the future potential of neuroplasticity and how breakthroughs in science and technology could reshape human health, cognitive abilities, and overall well-being.

Advances in Neuroscience research

The future of neuroplasticity research is closely tied to advancements in neuroscience, including cutting-edge techniques in brain imaging, neuromodulation, and molecular biology. These innovations will allow scientists to map brain changes with greater precision, manipulate neuroplasticity at the cellular level, and develop personalized interventions.

1. Brain Mapping and neural circuitry

Current technologies such as functional magnetic resonance imaging (fMRI) and diffusion tensor imaging (DTI) already allow researchers to observe changes in brain connectivity and plasticity in real-time. As these technologies become more sophisticated, future research will provide a clearer picture of how different neural circuits adapt over time and how they relate to behavior, learning, and recovery from injury.

Connectomics: The emerging field of connectomics aims to map all the neural connections in the brain, known as the connectome. By understanding how these networks are wired and how they change over time, scientists could develop targeted therapies to enhance or repair specific brain functions.

Personalized neuroplasticity: Future advancements in brain mapping may enable personalized approaches to neuroplasticity. By analyzing an individual's unique brain connectivity patterns, scientists could create tailored interventions to optimize learning, rehabilitation, or cognitive enhancement.

2. Neuromodulation techniques

Neuromodulation involves altering brain activity through electrical, magnetic, or chemical stimulation, and it is already being used in treatments for conditions like depression, Parkinson's disease, and epilepsy. In the future, more refined neuromodulation techniques could be used to enhance neuroplasticity for a wide range of applications.

Transcranial magnetic stimulation (TMS): TMS is a non-invasive technique that uses magnetic fields to stimulate specific regions of the brain. Future advances in TMS could allow for more precise targeting of brain areas involved in learning, memory, and rehabilitation, potentially accelerating recovery or cognitive training.

Deep brain stimulation (DBS): Currently used to treat movement disorders such as Parkinson's disease, DBS involves the implantation of electrodes that stimulate certain brain areas. As research continues, DBS could be used to promote neuroplasticity in other areas, including cognitive and emotional functions.

Transcranial direct current stimulation (TDCS): TDCS involves applying a low electrical current to the scalp to modulate brain activity. Future research may enhance the effectiveness of TDCS for improving learning, memory, and even creative thinking by fine-tuning its application.

Neuroplasticity and Artificial Intelligence

The intersection of neuroplasticity and artificial intelligence (AI) represents a promising frontier. As we learn more about how the brain adapts and learns, AI systems can be designed to replicate human-like learning processes. Additionally, neuroplasticity could inform the development of brain-computer interfaces (BCIs), creating a seamless interaction between the human brain and machines.

1. AI models inspired by Neuroplasticity

AI is increasingly being modeled after the human brain, with neural networks designed to simulate the brain's ability to learn and adapt through neuroplasticity. The future of AI may include systems that are even more sophisticated, capable of not only learning from experience but also reconfiguring their "neural" connections in response to new information, much like the human brain.

Neural networks and machine learning: AI neural networks are already inspired by the way neurons in the human brain communicate. In the future, AI could mimic the brain's capacity for lifelong learning, adapting to new inputs and conditions without needing to start from scratch.

Neuro-inspired AI: Advances in our understanding of neuroplasticity may lead to the development of AI systems that are capable of emulating the flexibility and efficiency of the human brain. These systems could be used in various fields, from medicine to autonomous systems.

2. Brain-Computer Interfaces (BCIs)

BCIs represent the next step in integrating neuroplasticity with technology. These systems allow for direct communication between the brain and external devices, such as prosthetics, computers, or even AI systems. In the future, BCIs could enable individuals to control machines with their thoughts, enhance cognitive abilities, or even restore lost functions by harnessing neuroplasticity.

Neurorehabilitation: BCIs are already showing promise in neurorehabilitation, particularly for patients with paralysis or neurological damage. By connecting the brain to external devices, BCIs can promote neural rewiring, allowing patients to regain control of movement through thought alone.

Cognitive enhancement: Future BCIs may be able to augment human cognitive abilities by directly stimulating or interacting with brain regions involved in memory, learning, or problem-solving. These technologies could revolutionize education, work, and daily life.

Neuroplasticity and Mental Health

As our understanding of neuroplasticity deepens, new treatments for mental health conditions are likely to emerge. The brain's capacity to rewire itself in response to emotional, cognitive, and environmental inputs can be leveraged to treat conditions such as depression, anxiety, PTSD, and more. Future treatments will likely focus on enhancing positive neuroplastic changes through a combination of therapy, medication, and neurostimulation.

1. Psychedelic-Assisted Therapy

Psychedelic compounds such as psilocybin, MDMA, and LSD are gaining attention for their potential to promote neuroplasticity and treat mental health conditions. Early research suggests that these compounds may induce neurogenesis, or the growth of new neurons, as well as synaptogenesis, the formation of new synaptic connections. In combination with psychotherapy, these substances could offer a new way to treat conditions like PTSD, depression, and addiction.

Neuroplasticity and healing: Psychedelic-assisted therapy may work by enhancing neuroplasticity, allowing individuals to break free from negative thought patterns, trauma, and behaviors. This could lead to lasting changes in brain circuits that regulate mood, cognition, and emotion.

Future research: As more clinical trials are conducted, psychedelic-assisted therapy could become a mainstream option for mental health treatment, offering a new way to harness neuroplasticity for emotional and psychological healing.

2. Digital Mental Health Interventions

Digital platforms that offer mental health support, such as cognitive-behavioral therapy (CBT) apps and mindfulness training, are already helping millions of people manage conditions like anxiety and depression. In the future, these platforms may evolve to incorporate personalized neuroplasticity-enhancing exercises tailored to an individual's brain activity patterns.

Customized interventions: Using AI and brain imaging, future digital mental health platforms could analyze brain function and provide real-time feedback on exercises that promote positive neuroplastic changes in mood regulation, stress resilience, and emotional control.

Neuroplasticity-driven therapy: With advancements in wearable EEG and other monitoring technologies, mental health treatments could become more precise, allowing individuals to track their brain activity and adjust their behavior to foster neuroplasticity that supports well-being.

Ethical Considerations and Neuroplasticity

As we move toward a future where neuroplasticity can be manipulated through technology, therapies, and interventions, ethical questions arise. The ability to shape brain function opens up possibilities for cognitive enhancement, mental health treatment, and even personality modification, but it also raises concerns about privacy, consent, and equitable access.

1. Cognitive Enhancement and Equity

If technologies like BCIs, neuromodulation, or cognitive-enhancing drugs become widely available, there is a risk that access to these innovations may be limited to those who can afford them. This could exacerbate existing inequalities in education, work, and overall quality of life.

Access to neuroplasticity-based treatments: Ensuring that all individuals have access to the benefits of neuroplasticity-enhancing technologies will be a key ethical challenge in the future. Policymakers will need to consider how to make these treatments widely available without creating social or economic disparities.

2. Privacy and Brain Data

As brain-computer interfaces and neuroimaging technologies become more advanced, they may also raise concerns about privacy. The ability to monitor or even manipulate brain activity could potentially be misused if safeguards are not put in place.

Brain data protection: Protecting the privacy of individuals' brain data will be crucial as we enter an era where such data could be collected and analyzed for therapeutic or commercial purposes. Ensuring that individuals have control over their brain data and how it is used will be essential for maintaining ethical standards in neuroplasticity research and applications.

Chapter 14: Conclusion

The Boundless Potential of Neuroplasticity

The future of neuroplasticity is filled with incredible potential. From revolutionary therapies for neurological conditions to cognitive enhancement and AI innovations, the ability to understand and harness the brain's adaptive capabilities will reshape human health, learning, and society. As we venture into this new frontier, it will be important to navigate the ethical, social, and technical challenges that arise, ensuring that the benefits of neuroplasticity are accessible to all while safeguarding individual rights and well-being. The future of neuroplasticity promises to be as adaptable and dynamic as the human brain itself.

In the final chapter, we bring together the core ideas explored throughout this book to highlight the transformative power of neuroplasticity. We will recap its vital role in shaping human potential, examine the endless possibilities that a plastic brain presents, and provide actionable insights on how to embrace and foster neuroplasticity in daily life for cognitive and emotional well-being.

Recap of Neuroplasticity's Role in Human Potential

Neuroplasticity—the brain's incredible ability to reorganize itself throughout life—forms the foundation of human potential. It allows us to learn new skills, recover from injuries, overcome psychological challenges, and adapt to the ever-changing world around us. The concept of neuroplasticity challenges the outdated notion that the brain is fixed or limited by age. Instead, it shows that with the right stimuli, the brain can continuously grow and evolve.

Throughout this book, we've explored how neuroplasticity influences every facet of life:

Learning and Memory: Neuroplasticity enables us to absorb information, retain memories, and refine our knowledge and skills. Whether learning a new language, musical instrument, or professional skill, neuroplasticity is at the heart of the process.

Recovery and Rehabilitation: Neuroplasticity offers hope in the context of recovery from brain injuries, strokes, or degenerative conditions. Through targeted interventions such as physical therapy, cognitive exercises, and neuromodulation, the brain can rewire itself to compensate for damaged areas.

Emotional Regulation and Mental Health: The plasticity of emotional circuits allows us to reshape our reactions to stress, trauma, and negative thought patterns. Therapeutic practices like cognitive-behavioral therapy (CBT), mindfulness, and even psychedelic-assisted therapies leverage neuroplasticity to foster emotional resilience and psychological healing.

Cognitive Enhancement: From brain training apps to brain-computer interfaces (BCIs), the future holds exciting possibilities for using neuroplasticity to enhance cognitive abilities, extend brain longevity, and unlock greater creativity and innovation.

In summary, neuroplasticity is a powerful biological mechanism that underpins our ability to change, grow, and improve. Understanding its role unlocks a deeper appreciation for the potential each person holds to shape their brain and life experience.

The endless possibilities of a plastic brain

A plastic brain presents boundless possibilities for human growth and transformation. With an understanding of how neuroplasticity works, we can reshape our mental and physical abilities far beyond the limitations we once thought existed. This section emphasizes the limitless applications and implications of neuroplasticity.

1. Lifelong learning and skill mastery

One of the most exciting aspects of neuroplasticity is its persistence throughout life. It proves that the brain never stops learning or evolving, regardless of age. This means that older adults can continue acquiring new skills and expanding their cognitive capacities. Whether mastering a new language in your 70s or learning how to code in middle age, the plasticity of the brain ensures that the human mind remains dynamic and adaptable.

2. Overcoming adversity and resilience

Neuroplasticity is also the engine behind our resilience. It allows the brain to recover from trauma—whether physical or emotional—by rewiring neural circuits to adapt to new circumstances. People can overcome personal challenges, from anxiety and depression to overcoming physical disabilities, by harnessing the brain's capacity to heal and form new pathways. The stories of stroke survivors who regain mobility, trauma victims who recover emotional balance, or individuals who overcome addictions through neuroplasticity-driven therapies show the vast scope of this power.

Cognitive enhancement and innovation

As we look ahead, neuroplasticity may play a pivotal role in advancing human cognition. Technologies like brain training platforms, BCIs, and neurofeedback are just the beginning of what's possible. In the future, neuroplasticity could help extend human brain performance beyond its natural limits, promoting creativity, problem-solving, and innovation in ways we can only imagine.

AI and neural networks: The interplay between neuroplasticity and artificial intelligence may revolutionize not only technology but how humans interact with machines and learn. The potential for AI to mimic and enhance neuroplastic processes opens new doors for collaboration between human intelligence and technology.

Personalized brain interventions: The emerging field of neuroplasticity-enhancing interventions tailored to individual brain activity could lead to breakthroughs in personalized learning, mental health treatments, and cognitive therapies.

4. A Future of brain flexibility

With neuroplasticity, the future of human potential is open-ended. Our ability to continually shape our brains means that innovation, creativity, recovery, and personal transformation will know no bounds. Whether through self-directed learning, targeted rehabilitation, or enhanced cognition through technology, the plastic brain provides humanity with the tools to reach new heights.

How to embrace and foster Neuroplasticity in daily life

While neuroplasticity offers a vast range of possibilities, it is up to individuals to take proactive steps to cultivate it in their lives. By adopting habits and practices that stimulate brain plasticity, anyone can unlock their brain's potential for growth, adaptation, and emotional well-being. Here are some practical ways to embrace and foster neuroplasticity in your daily life:

1. Lifelong learning and curiosity

One of the most effective ways to promote neuroplasticity is to keep learning. By challenging yourself with new knowledge and skills, you stimulate your brain to form new neural connections.

Learn new skills: Engage in activities that challenge you mentally, such as learning a musical instrument, picking up a new language, or mastering a hobby like painting or cooking.

Stay curious: Keep exploring new topics and areas of interest. Whether through reading, traveling, or engaging in discussions, staying curious keeps your brain engaged and adaptable.

2. Mindfulness and meditation

Mindfulness practices, such as meditation, have been shown to foster positive neuroplasticity by strengthening regions of the brain involved in attention, emotional regulation, and stress management.

Daily mindfulness practice: Integrating mindfulness meditation into your daily routine can help reduce stress, improve emotional regulation, and enhance cognitive focus, all while promoting neuroplastic changes in the brain.

Mindful learning: Practice mindful engagement with tasks, focusing fully on the present moment. This helps to strengthen the brain's attention circuits.

3. Physical exercise and movement

Physical exercise is one of the most powerful ways to stimulate neuroplasticity. Exercise increases blood flow to the brain, promotes the growth of new neurons, and strengthens the neural circuits that support memory, learning, and emotional health.

Aerobic exercise: Activities like walking, jogging, swimming, and cycling boost brain health by promoting neurogenesis in the hippocampus, the region of the brain associated with memory.

Skill-based exercise: Engaging in activities that require coordination and learning new physical skills, such as dancing, martial arts, or sports, can enhance neuroplasticity by challenging motor and cognitive functions simultaneously.

4. Cognitive training and mental puzzles

Engaging in mental exercises, such as puzzles, strategy games, and brain training apps, helps to keep the brain sharp and encourages neuroplasticity.

Brain games: Play games that challenge your problem-solving abilities, such as chess, Sudoku, or crossword puzzles. These activities keep your brain flexible and improve cognitive function.

Digital brain training: Apps like Lumosity and Peak offer structured cognitive exercises designed to enhance memory, attention, and reasoning skills by promoting neuroplasticity.

5. Social interaction and emotional connection

Human connection plays a significant role in promoting neuroplasticity. Engaging in meaningful social interactions and building emotional bonds helps to strengthen neural circuits related to empathy, communication, and emotional regulation.

Build relationships: Make time for social activities and cultivate meaningful connections with friends, family, and communities. Social engagement keeps the brain active and adaptable.

Practice empathy and active listening: Engage deeply with others by practicing empathy and attentive listening. This fosters emotional plasticity, helping the brain adapt to social cues and relationships.

6. Healthy sleep and nutrition

Both sleep and nutrition play crucial roles in maintaining brain health and supporting neuroplasticity. Sleep helps consolidate memories and new learning, while a balanced diet provides the nutrients necessary for brain function.

Prioritize sleep: Ensure you get enough restorative sleep each night, as sleep is critical for memory consolidation and cognitive recovery.

Brain-boosting foods: Eat a diet rich in brain-healthy nutrients, including omega-3 fatty acids (found in fish and flaxseeds), antioxidants (found in berries and dark leafy greens), and vitamins that support cognitive function (such as B vitamins, found in whole grains and legumes).

Xxxxxxxxxxxxxxx

Final word

As we came to the end of this journey through the mind's remarkable ability to transform, it's clear that neuroplasticity holds the key to unlocking profound changes in our lives. The brain is not a fixed organ, but a dynamic, malleable force, constantly reshaping itself in response to how we think, feel, and act. This discovery opens up a great world of possibilities, reminding us that change is not only possible—it is inevitable if we choose to engage with it consciously.

The beauty of neuroplasticity is that it empowers each of us to break free from old patterns, heal from trauma, and cultivate new habits that serve our greatest potential. Whether it's overcoming limiting beliefs, learning new skills, or fostering resilience, the brain's capacity to rewire itself offers endless opportunities for growth.

As you move forward, remember that your thoughts, behaviors, and emotions are the architects of your brain's future. By choosing positive, intentional actions, you are shaping not only your present but also the very structure of your mind. With this knowledge, you hold the power to design a life of purpose, joy, and limitless possibility.

The science of neuroplasticity shows us that we are never too old, too stuck, or too damaged to change. We are all capable of growth, no matter where we start. The journey may not always be easy, but it is always worth it. So embrace this power, trust in the process, and step boldly into the future using your mind as the greatest tool for creating the life you desire.

Remember mind is the software for the hardware called brain. They complement each other so well that the separation of one renders the very existence of the other questionable.

All the best!! **KV Shan**